MINDMASTERS

THE DATA-DRIVEN SCIENCE OF
PREDICTING AND CHANGING
HUMAN BEHAVIOR

MINDMASTERS

SANDRA MATZ

HARVARD BUSINESS REVIEW PRESS
BOSTON, MASSACHUSETTS

Library of Congress Cataloging-in-Publication Data

Names: Matz, Sandra C., author.
Title: Mindmasters : the data-driven science of predicting and changing human behavior / Sandra Matz.
Description: Boston, Massachusetts : Harvard Business Review Press, [2025] | Includes index.
Identifiers: LCCN 2024023257 (print) | LCCN 2024023258 (ebook) | ISBN 9781647826314 (hardcover) | ISBN 9781647826321 (epub)
Subjects: LCSH: Psychology—Research—Methodology. | Psychology—Technological innovations. | Technological innovations—Psychological aspects. | Human behavior—Research. | Data mining—Social aspects.
Classification: LCC BF76.5 .M373 2025 (print) | LCC BF76.5 (ebook) | DDC 150.72—dc23/eng/20240905
LC record available at https://lccn.loc.gov/2024023257
LC ebook record available at https://lccn.loc.gov/2024023258

ISBN: 978-1-64782-631-4
eISBN: 978-1-64782-632-1

To Moran and Ben, whose love and laughter
fill my life with magic every day.

CONTENTS

MINDMASTERS

The Digital Village

I had begged my boyfriend for weeks to let me ride his motorcycle. A Suzuki Bandit 600. In a deep, shimmering red. It was beautiful.

We loved to take the bike on adventures together. Up the serpentine roads of the mountains surrounding the small village I grew up in, and through the curvy roads of the countryside. But I was tired of being in the back. I wanted to be in the driver's seat.

When he finally agreed to let me try, I found an abandoned military airfield nearby.

His instructions were simple: "Let's sit on the bike first. You in the front and me in the back. And then I'll explain." I was enthralled but nervous, too. I was only fifteen, and I didn't have a license. "Don't worry," he assured me, "I'm sitting right behind you."

I don't know exactly what happened next. I remember that we somehow rolled into the grass on the side of the airfield. When I tried to pull the bike back out, I must have accidentally twisted the throttle and let the clutch snatch.

A few seconds later, the front wheel of the motorcycle rose into the air like a rearing horse. My boyfriend was thrown off the back (so much for "I'm sitting right behind you"), and I sped off without the slightest idea of how to control the bike.

Without thinking, I pulled and pushed the bike's handlebars, trying to keep my balance. For what felt like an eternity, I swerved left, right, left again, before I came crashing down on one side, sliding for a few feet before coming to a stop.

We were lucky. Neither of us got injured. And nobody had witnessed the accident. But there was a problem: we were in the middle of nowhere and the bike wouldn't start.

After weighing our options, I sat down on the grass to calm my nerves, took a deep breath, and hit the call button on my phone. Part of me was hoping no one would pick up. With every ring, my heart started beating louder, my mind racing. When I was almost ready to hang up, my dad answered the phone.

"Hi, Dad, . . . uh . . . we had a motorcycle accident. But don't worry, we were going slow, and we're both fine."

"It was you driving, right?"

In addition to a serious conversation with my parents (who were actually surprisingly cool about it), I had to pay for the repairs. A full year's salary of tutoring gone. Painful, but not the worst part.

The minute we dropped the bike at the local repair shop, the news about my misfortune spread through my village like wildfire. It was the perfect story. Not just because I was fifteen and didn't have a license. I also happened to be the daughter of a local police officer.

There was no place to hide. The next day, on my way to the school bus, Mr. Werner from across the street waved me over to inquire if I was doing OK. He had heard about the crash. I got trapped in a ten-minute recounting of his own teenage offenses.

A few houses down, Ms. Bauer looked up from weeding the little garden in the front of her house, shaking her head. How could I be so irresponsible? She had always thought of me as a smart girl.

The motorcycle crash was no longer my own private embarrassment. Everyone—and I mean *everyone*—knew my business.

The Village Paradox

Welcome to Vögisheim! A tiny village in the southwest corner of Germany surrounded by pretty vineyards, fields, and rolling hills. Population: five hundred. Restaurants: two. Churches: one. Shops: zero.

I was born and raised there. Just like my mom, her mom, and her mom's mom. I lived there for the first eighteen years of my life—and for what felt like an eternity as a teenager craving the stimulation of busier places. Vögisheim is where I spoke my first words, took my first steps, fell in love for the first time, had my first heartbreak, decided to travel the world, and eventually embarked on a journey to study psychology.

As in any small village, the other 499 residents of Vögisheim didn't just know about my motorcycle crash. They knew every little detail of my life. They knew that I loved listening to the Ramones, that my favorite place for weekend nights was the local pirate bar, and that I simply couldn't stand my geography teacher.

Those details alone might not have felt that intrusive. But, as if I were a human puzzle, my neighbors put the pieces of my existence together to construct an intimate picture of my inner mental life: my hopes, fears, dreams, and aspirations. They seemed to *truly* know me. Which allowed them to do what village neighbors do best . . . offer (un)solicited advice and interfere with my personal life.

For me, this meant two things. On the one hand, I felt supported by a community of people who understood me. They knew I was ambitious and longed for a life outside the village. So, when the time came for me to figure out what to do after high school, they were there to offer advice and opportunities; they passed on my curriculum vitae to friends and helped me decide whether a gap year was the right choice for me.

On the other hand, I felt exposed and manipulated by the same community. It was a poorly kept secret that I had a hard time saying no to people. This made me an easy target for anyone who needed a favor. Moving apartments? Ask Sandra. In need of a ride home from the club? Ask Sandra (if the vehicle of choice wasn't a motorcycle, of course).

Growing up being seen by others was a blessing and a curse at the same time.

From the Village to the World

I left Vögisheim after graduating from high school and today live in New York City where I am a professor at Columbia University.

A difference like day and night. I barely know my neighbors. And they barely know me. We say hi to each other when we meet in the corridor. But they don't know what I do for work. They don't know my friends and family. And they certainly don't know anything about my deepest fears or aspirations.

But as it turns out, you don't have to live in a small, rural community to have someone watch and influence every step you take and choice you make. That's because we all have *digital neighbors*.

Think of it this way: the data-crawling digital equivalent to my sixty-year-old neighbor Klaus reads my Facebook messages, observes which news I read and share on X/Twitter, collects my credit card purchases, tracks my whereabouts via my smartphone's GPS sensor, and records my facial expressions and casual encounters using some 50 million public cameras across the United States.

In the same way my neighbors became expert snoopers and puppeteers over time, computers can translate seemingly mundane, innocuous information about *what we do* into highly intimate insights about *who we are* and ultimately prescriptions of *what we should do*.

I call this process of influencing people's thoughts, feelings, and behaviors based on their predicted psychological characteristics *psychological targeting*. And I've been studying it—and practicing it—for over a decade now.

My colleagues and I have published numerous articles showing how computers—powered by machine learning and AI—can get to know you intimately. It doesn't matter which psychological trait or data source you pick. For example, algorithms can tell whether you are excited, sad, sociable, or anxious by tapping into your phone's microphone or camera. They can predict your income from your social media posts. And they can tell whether you are likely to develop depression or suffer from schizophrenia by tracking your GPS location.

But that's only half the story. I've spent most of my career tackling the glaring "So what?" question. What does it mean that computers can peek into our psychology and understand what lies below the surface of the behaviors they can observe? What does it mean for you and me? And for society at large? It doesn't take much imagination to understand that psychological targeting, in the wrong hands, could be a powerful weapon.

When I was a teenager, I struggled with low self-esteem. I wanted nothing more than to belong and be liked. But it was my best friend who was popular, not me. I became very good at hiding my self-doubts from the other people in the village, putting on a facade that bordered on arrogance. On the outside, I was strong and confident. Inside, I doubted myself. I shared these feelings in my diary.

If I were a teenager today, I would probably ask Google for advice. "How can I become more popular?" "How do I feel better about myself?" These questions would build up in my search history. And the resulting profile could easily be used against me. In 2017, Facebook was accused of predicting depression among teenagers and selling this information to advertisers.[1] No easier target than insecure, struggling teens. Pretty gloomy.

But let's look at this in a more positive light. What if we could use psychological targeting to help millions of people lead healthier and happier lives? My research, for example, has been used to predict and prevent college dropouts, guide low-income individuals toward better financial decisions, and detect early signs of depression.

Yes, that's right. The very thing I accused Facebook of doing in the "gloomy" section could also be a real opportunity. Depression affects approximately 280 million people around the world. Every year, about 1 million of them commit suicide. That's more people dying from the consequences of depression than from homicide, terror attacks, and natural disasters together.

What makes these numbers particularly upsetting is that depression is treatable. The problem is that many people are never diagnosed. Even if they are, the diagnosis often arrives too late. It is much harder to fight your way back from the bottom of the valley than from the initial descent.

What if, instead of selling you out to advertisers, we used the insights into your mental health profile to build an early warning system? GPS records or tweets could alert you to changes in your behavior that resemble patterns observed in other people suffering from depression. It's not only a chance to detect depressive symptoms early (before they develop into a full, clinical depression) but also to offer personalized advice or resources.

We might observe that you are not interacting with your friends as much anymore, or you're spending a lot more time at home than usual. Why not encourage you to reach out to a few of your friends or spend some time in the park nearby? And, if necessary, provide you with contact details of a few therapists in the area that might be of help.

Predicting and influencing mental health outcomes is merely one of many examples demonstrating the power of psychological targeting. What if we could make education more engaging, help people achieve their fitness goals, or facilitate a more constructive dialogue across the political divide?

For the better part of my academic career, I've felt somewhat helpless and lost in the tension between the perilous and promising sides of analyzing personal data. Was I in the camp of techno pessimists arguing that technology fails to deliver on its promises and actively harms humanity? Or was I in the camp of techno optimists who believe in a bright future where technology helps us become better versions of ourselves?

I often felt like a hypocrite—excited about new findings, with this nagging feeling that, in the wrong hands, those findings could have horrible consequences. Or vice versa, talking to media about the dangers of psychological profiling, while fearing I was backstabbing my students and industry partners who saw the potential promises of psychological profiling.

It wasn't until a Christmas trip back home (and after multiple rounds of mulled wine) that I realized how similar my current struggle was to my experience in the village—constantly torn between the desire to break free and the appreciation for what my community had to offer. The more I thought about this analogy (in a sober state), the more glaringly obvious it became.

I was dealing with a new manifestation of a tension that has been part of the human experience for centuries. How much of our private lives are we willing (or even happy) to disclose to those around us? How much of our privacy and autonomy are we willing to give up for the security and strength provided by the collective?

What this all comes down to is power. In the same way my neighbors had an easy time convincing me to do chores for them because they knew I was a crowd pleaser, understanding your psychological needs, preferences, and motivations gives others power over you. Power to influence your opinions, emotions, and ultimately behavior. Sometimes this is good; sometimes it's bad.

But life in the village taught me that whether we win or lose is—at least in part—up to us. Even though I never had full control over my life, I still managed to navigate the ups and downs. As a kid, I had no idea how the village operated. But over time, I learned more about the system I was embedded in. I understood people's motivations, figured out who was talking to whom, and learned who could be trusted with information.

Once I understood the game that was played and had a clear sense of what I wanted out of it, I learned to play it to my advantage. Suddenly, I was winning more than I was losing.

We need to do the same—and more—for the digital village. We need to understand the players that control the current data ecosystem, figure out how they use our personal data for and against us, and identify the leverage we have (or need) to come out on top.

But merely becoming better at playing the game won't be enough. We need to redesign it.

Redesigning the Data Game

I have argued that the tension we experience in today's data-driven world is the same as the one our ancestors experienced two thousand years ago, or the one I struggled with in my village. But that's not entirely true.

While I was exposed to the prying eyes of villagers (and maybe their friends in the adjacent villages looking for juicy gossip), our digital behavior today exposes us to the entire world. The rules of the game have changed.

Growing up in a village, my neighbors knew a lot about me. But trust me, I also knew a lot about them. I knew who was struggling with alcoholism, who was unhappy in their marriage, and who was evading taxes. We all played the game as equals. We all paid the price, and we all benefited.

Today's data game looks nothing like this. Its rules are opaque, and its playing field is highly tilted. There are a few people and organizations that know an awful lot about many of us and that benefit greatly from this knowledge. We may get certain things from the exchange (free-of-charge search engines and social media, for instance), but we don't get reciprocal knowledge about the people and organizations that track us so zealously.

Even though the game we play in the digital village might have slightly different rules, the best starting point to stack the deck in our favor remains the same. We need to understand what novel predictive technologies such as psychological targeting are capable of and collectively decide which applications are conducive to a thriving society, and which aren't. Once we do, it is within our control to design a system that amplifies the positive sides of psychological targeting and makes it work *for* us, instead of *against* us.

Mindmasters is an invitation to do just that—an invitation to join an informed, nuanced discussion of psychological targeting. Cases like Cambridge Analytica's alleged interference in the 2016 US presidential election (a story I helped break and will talk more about in chapter 5) have caught the public eye and informed much of the public debate on the topic.

My goal for *Mindmasters* is to pull back the curtain, separate narrative from facts, and offer a science-based account of psychological targeting. I will do so across three parts, each touching on an important puzzle piece of the overall process.

Part 1 takes you on a journey through how computers learn to translate your digital footprints into intimate predictions of who you are: your personality, sexual orientation, political ideology, mental health, moral values, and more. We'll open a digital window into our psyche by entering the worlds of deliberately shared identity claims (e.g., Facebook likes, social media posts, and pictures) and innocuous behavioral residue (e.g., Google searches, credit card data, and GPS records). And we'll explore the role of contextual cues in giving away information about who we are at any given point in time.

As we open the black box and look under the hood of some of the AI-powered predictive models that my colleagues and I have built over the years, you will realize that it doesn't take rocket science to translate what we do online to who we are on the inside.

To be clear, computers don't necessarily need to translate your behavior into psychological profiles to know you intimately and interfere with your choices. Many of the potential benefits and dangers I discuss in later parts of the book apply to the use of personal data more broadly. But cases like Cambridge Analytica have caught the public imagination because they allow us to relate to our data in a fundamentally human way. You don't think of yourself as a combination of spending records, GPS-tracked longitude and latitude coordinates, and Google searches. You think of yourself as extroverted or introverted, liberal or conversative, and cooperative or competitive.

Part 2 directly builds on the insights from part 1 to discuss the glaring "So what?" question. Why should we care about the proliferation of technologies like psychological targeting? What does it mean for us—and society at large—that algorithms can decode the inner mental lives of millions of people and alter the way they think, feel and behave? Should we be scared or elated?

I will argue that we should be both. As the tech historian Melvin Kranzberg famously said: "Technology is neither good nor bad, nor is it neutral."[2] The exact same mechanisms can be used to accomplish diametrically opposed goals. By tapping into your psychology, I can get you to buy products you might not need, but also to save more money for a rainy day. I can exploit your emotional vulnerabilities but also help you overcome them. And I can reinforce your existing worldviews but also encourage and enable you to expand them.

The impact of psychological targeting ultimately depends on *us* and the choices *we* make. At its worst, psychological targeting manipulates, exploits, and discriminates. At its best, it engages, educates, and empowers.

As advanced AI technology—including generative AI—makes the creation and targeting of hyperpersonalized content easier than ever before, we need a clear vision for how to amplify the opportunities afforded by psychological targeting while mitigating its risks. That's what part 3 of the book is all about. How do we redesign the data game to create a better future for all of us?

I will argue that creating this future requires us to return to the village. Not literally. No need to pack your bags, take the kids, and move to your version of Vögisheim. I'm talking about small village-style communities designed to help you manage your personal data. Entities that are legally obliged (e.g., through fiduciary responsibilities) to act in the best interest of their members. A data trust or data co-op.

Today's data landscape is simply too complex to fight this fight alone. I might have been able to look after myself in the game we played in the village, but I don't stand a chance in today's global arena. And neither do you. No one has the knowledge, time, and energy to manage their personal data all by themselves.

We need allies. Like-minded people who have similar interests and share the same goals. Expectant mothers, for example, sharing their medical and biometric data with one another to figure out the best nutrition for a safe pregnancy. Or educators pooling performance data from their classrooms to develop more effective teaching strategies.

Unlike village neighbors, your digital allies don't have to live in the same place as you. Technology solves that problem (and many more, as I will describe in more detail later). With about eight billion people around the world, you will eventually find someone with the same problems and values as you.

What I am suggesting isn't simply a return to the old ways of the village. It's not just a one-to-one translation of tried-and-tested solutions to a new problem. The game we play online today is different from the game I played in Vögisheim, and so are the solutions. The good news is that if we get this right, we might be able to have it all: the benefits that come with letting others into our lives without the costs of losing our privacy and self-determination.

Although *Mindmasters* centers around data and technology, it is, at its core, an exploration of the human experience: how we want to both reveal and conceal, how we gain and lose by letting others into our lives, and how new technologies like psychological targeting require us to rethink the social contract. It's as much an attempt at sharing my learnings with you as it is an invitation for you to join the conversation. To become part of redesigning the game.

PART ONE

DATA IS A WINDOW INTO OUR PSYCHOLOGY

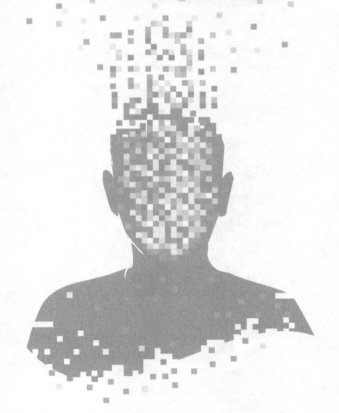

1

Decoding Our Psychology

I t's 8 a.m. on a Monday morning. As usual, it's not my alarm clock that wakes me up, but my dog Milou licking my face (a bit gross, I know). I give her a squeeze, push her to the side, and reach for my phone.

I check my WhatsApp and Facebook, scan my emails, and catch up on the latest news on CNN. Before taking Milou out, I put on my Fitbit to make sure that every step I take counts toward my daily goal of ten thousand steps. I'm tempted to tie my Fitbit to her collar, but resist. Don't judge me. According to my friend Alice Moon's research, I'm not the only one who cheats on their step count.

Milou and I go for a walk across campus where she can run around off leash and harass the early-riser students, who love the free cuddles.

After a quick shower at home, I grab my phone and wallet and head out to work. On the way, I pick up a matcha latte and a croissant from the deli around the corner. I arrive at the office shortly before 9 a.m.

In less than one hour, I have generated millions of digital footprints. On a server somewhere around the world, there are now digital records of the messages I have sent and received (incoming: cute pictures of my nieces; outgoing: cute pictures of Milou), the fact that I checked in with Facebook from my home location, spent about ten minutes reading five different articles on CNN's website, I took about two thousand steps walking across the Columbia University campus in Manhattan, and got an unhealthy deli breakfast.

In addition, the sensors in my phone have registered that there was physical activity starting from 8 a.m. and have tracked my GPS location continuously. The cameras on the corners of streets, outside the deli, and inside the elevators have collected visuals of me, telling them exactly where I have been at any point in time, whether I was alone or accompanied, and whether I looked happy or not (at 8 a.m., I rarely do).

Like the average person, you and I generate about six gigabytes of data every hour.[1] Every hour! Just imagine how many USB drives you would need to save all the data that accumulates over the course of your lifespan. And that is just *your* data.

Worldwide, there are now an estimated 149 zettabytes of data (that is 149,000,000,000,000,000,000,000 bytes), with numbers doubling every year. If you were to store all this data on CD-ROMs and stack them on top of each other, you would reach far beyond the moon. In fact, some have suggested that today there are almost as many digital pieces of data as there are stars in the vast universe. Romantic, isn't it?

Each of these data points represents a little puzzle piece of who we are. My Spotify playlist, for example, reveals that I love techno and Taylor Swift. My credit card history, that I enjoy traveling. And my GPS records, that I love to go for long walks in the park.

Individually, these pieces aren't that meaningful. Just like in a puzzle, you start with a pile of disconnected chaos. But once you put the pieces together, you gradually begin to see the full picture and understand its meaning. The same is true for data. Once connected, our digital traces provide a rich picture of our personal habits, preferences, needs, and motivations. In short: our psychology.

The Internet Knows You Better Than Your Spouse Does

In 2015, the *Financial Times* ran an article with the provocative headline, "Facebook understands you better than your spouse." Sounds like the opening to a dystopian science fiction novel? Nope. It's the result of a real scientific study published by my former colleagues at the University of Cambridge.[2]

The research team led by Youyou Wu had built a series of machine learning models that could translate a person's Facebook likes into personality profiles. The results were astonishing: after observing just ten likes from someone's Facebook profile, their model was able to judge a user's personality better than their work colleagues. Sixty-five likes? It knew users better than someone's friends. A hundred-twenty likes? Better than family members. And three hundred? Better than their spouse.

When my colleagues first told me about their findings, I was sure they had made a mistake (and so were they, initially). Clearly, there was a bug in the code.

But there wasn't. My colleagues were right. Seven years later, I am still amazed by their findings. We call our spouses our "other halves" for a reason. They often have years of data on us. They plan, experience, and live life with us every day. And yet, with access to just about three hundred of your Facebook likes, a computer can know you just as well or even better.

This puts the snooping skills of my village neighbors to shame. Even the most curious among them probably knew far less about me than any semiskilled computer scientist or engineer with access to the right data. Today, a fifteen-year-old kid in the basement of their parents' home could figure out more about me than all my village neighbors together.

But how do computers become such master snoopers? How do they make sense of the vast, unstructured sea of digital footprints to paint a picture of the person behind it? The simple answer is: they observe and learn (yup, big shocker, that's why it's called machine learning).

Let me illustrate this process with an example that has absolutely nothing to do with computers or algorithms. My main protagonists are chickens. Baby chicks, to be precise.

A Villager's Guide to Machine Learning

Have you ever heard of sexing? Don't worry: this topic is safe for work.

Chick sexing refers to the practice of distinguishing between female chicks (pullets) and male chicks (cockerels). Large commercial hatcheries use it to separate the high-value female chicks from the male chicks almost immediately after birth.

While the female chicks are used for egg production, the male chicks are usually killed to reduce unnecessary cost for the hatchery (and suddenly becoming a vegetarian doesn't sound so bad anymore).

The act of sexing is done by experienced personnel—sexers—who have to decide within a few seconds whether a chick is female or male by examining the vent in the chick's rear (known as "vent sexing").

As it turns out, this is not an easy task. The genitals of newborn chicken are almost indistinguishable by eye, and there are so many exceptions that it's practically impossible for even the most experienced sexers to explain their decision-making process. After years of training, they simply know. But how do they learn to distinguish between male and female chicks in the first place? Trial and error.

Imagine you have just started as a sexer in a major hatchery. It's day one and you are excited to start your new job. But there is no instruction manual, no fifty-page report or PowerPoint deck to introduce you to the wonders of chick sexing. Instead, you are teamed up with an experienced chick sexer who stands right next to you, quietly observing.

You pick up the first chick and examine its rear. Of course, you have no idea; it's your first day at work and your experience with chick vents has been, um, limited.

You shrug and put the chick into the pullets bin. Your mentor says, "Yes." Success. You pick up the next one and after a short examination put it in the cockerels bin. Your mentor says, "No."

Your first day at work won't feel very satisfying—your chance of making the right choice will likely hover just above 50 percent (that's a coin flip). But after a couple of weeks of running through the trial-and-error game with your mentor, your brain will have been trained to accurately distinguish between male and female chicks. You have become a sexing master! Just like your mentor, the rules guiding your decision-making might be too complex to articulate, but you have nevertheless internalized them.

Computers learn in the same way: trial and error. You throw a lot of examples at them and give feedback on whether their predictions are right or wrong. Doing so will gradually allow the algorithm to learn how the input (a chick's rear or a set of Facebook likes) is related to the output (a chick's gender or a user's personality traits).

Do your Facebook likes include content about Oscar Wilde, Leonardo da Vinci, and Plato? You're probably intellectually curious and open-minded. Accounting, MyCalendar, and national law enforcement? Most likely organized and reliable.

The more data you have to run through the trial-and-error game, the better the computer will become at turning educated guesses into highly accurate predictions. That's exactly what my colleagues did when they conducted their man-versus-machine experiment. They collected a large dataset of over eighteen thousand Facebook users, combined their likes with self-reported personality profiles, and wrote a few lines of code to automate the trial-and-error learning process (a trivial task that can be done with user-friendly commercial software today).

In the next few chapters, I will take you on a journey through different types of digital footprints and show you how much they can reveal about who you are. Some of these footprints, such as your social media profiles, are created intentionally (chapter 2). Others, such as the GPS records extracted from your smartphone, are mere by-products of your interactions with technology (chapter 3).

But they all have one thing in common: they offer a fascinating window into your psychology—the aspects of your identity that define who you are beyond what is visible to the naked eye. We'll venture into the worlds of political ideology, sexual orientation, socioeconomic status, mental health, cognitive ability, personal values, and more.

But most of our time together will be spent in the world of personality traits. It's where most of the existing research lives, including my own. And it's also the world that has received the most public attention and scrutiny (think Cambridge Analytica).

Because personality is such a popular destination, I want to get us all on the same page about what to expect there—a crash course for aspiring master snoopers, if you want (if you know all about personality, feel free to skip ahead to chapter 2).

The Big Five Personality Traits

Like most people, you probably have an intuitive concept of personality that guides your everyday behavior and social interactions.

In my school, it was clear that Vera was the party animal, while I was, well, the nerdy geek who went home at 11 p.m. when everybody else was still out dancing.

In my village, we all explained the butcher's frequent outbursts of anger with his impulsive and irritable character. And at university, we all predicted that Anne would become a successful lawyer as a result of her competitive nature.

Although such lay theories of personality help us navigate our social world, they are often implicit and only loosely defined. You might not be able to fully explain why you think a particular person is irritable and you might not be consistent in your terminology.

Sometimes you might label the same behavior impulsive, other times grumpy or angry.

In contrast to lay theories, scientific models of personality provide a structured approach to describing how people differ from one another in the ways they think, feel, and behave. Rather than accounting for the full complexity of someone's identity, they provide pragmatic approximations of what most people are like.

The results of a personality test, for example, will tell you that my school friend Vera is highly extroverted. But you won't know if Vera is the kind of person who goes to parties to talk to other people, or if she mostly goes there to dance. Or maybe both.

Scientific personality models sacrifice a high level of granularity for a high level of consistency and comparability. You won't be able to understand all the nuances of who Vera is. But you will be able to directly compare her character to that of others.

The most popular scientific model of personality is the Big Five.[3] You might also know it as OCEAN model named after the five personality traits it measures: openness to experience, conscientiousness, extroversion, agreeableness, and neuroticism. I will give you the chance to take a short personality test in a minute. It will allow you to learn about your own personality profile before we embark on our master snooping tour.

But let me first add a little bit more color to the five traits. You can also see a summary in table 1-1.

Openness to experience: The Picasso trait

Openness to experience (or openness) refers to the extent to which people prefer novelty over convention. People scoring high on openness are intellectually curious, sensitive to beauty, individualistic, imaginative, and unconventional. You might find them engaged in philosophical discussions, traveling the world, exploring new restaurants, visiting a museum, writing poetry, or painting.

TABLE 1-1

The Big Five in a nutshell

Personality trait	Low	High
Openness	Practical; down-to-earth; traditional; conservative; preference for the familiar	Imaginative; curious; original/ creative; appreciation for art, beauty, and aesthetics; open-minded
Conscientiousness	Flexible, carefree, disorganized; unreliable; spontaneous	Organized; dependable; goal-oriented; detail-oriented; self-disciplined
Extroversion	Reserved; quiet; introspective; deliberate; solitary	Sociable; talkative; energetic; enthusiastic; assertive
Agreeableness	Critical; blunt; skeptical; competitive; independent-minded	Compassionate; cooperative; trusting; altruistic; diplomatic
Neuroticism	Calm; emotionally stable; resilient; confident; grounded	Anxious; emotional; sensitive; nervous; easily stressed

Source: Adapted from Gerald Matthews, Ian J. Deary, and Martha C. Whiteman, *Personality Traits* (Cambridge, UK: Cambridge University Press, 2003).

People scoring low on openness, on the other hand, are down-to-earth and more conservative in the values they hold (including politics). They might not get excited by the idea of traveling to new and unknown places, but instead prefer to return to their all-time favorite all-inclusive hotel on the Riviera.

The Spanish painter, sculptor, printmaker, ceramicist, stage designer, poet, and playwright Pablo Picasso is an excellent example of an open-minded personality. Regarded as one of the most talented artists of his time, and one of the most inspiring and influential figures of the twentieth century, Picasso experimented with a wide variety of artistic styles over the course of his career and gave birth to more novel forms of artistic expression than any other artist at the time (e.g., the collage or the Cubist movement). The quote "Others have seen what is and asked why. I have seen what could be and asked why not" perfectly captures Picasso's mix of intellectual curiosity, preference for novelty, and artistic interest, which also characterizes the personality trait of openness.

Conscientiousness: The Angela Merkel trait

Conscientiousness refers to the extent to which people prefer an organized or a flexible approach in life. It captures how we control, regulate, and direct our impulses.

People scoring high on conscientiousness are organized, reliable, perfectionists, and efficient. They tend to be good at following rules, resisting temptation, and sticking to schedules. And they love order. Everything needs to be in the right place. Everything needs to be perfect.

In contrast, people scoring low on conscientiousness are more spontaneous, impulsive, careless, absent-minded, or disorganized. They don't care as much about achievements and instead take a much more relaxed and spontaneous approach to life. They might wait until the last minute to study for an exam or plan their holiday on the way to the airport. And yes, they are the ones who regularly forget about their friends' birthdays or their own wedding anniversary.

I've heard some people call conscientiousness the German trait. I assume that's because it leaves you with the image of a meticulously organized and perfectionist person. The sort of person that organizes their socks according to color and stacks up books in alphabetical order. It's why I call it the Angela Merkel trait—always perfectly prepared and dependable (I should say that, sadly, this characteristic doesn't apply to all Germans).

Extroversion: The Lady Gaga trait

Extroversion refers to the extent to which people enjoy company and seek excitement and stimulation. It is marked by a pronounced engagement with the external world, versus being comfortable with one's own company.

People scoring high on extroversion can be described as energetic, active, talkative, sociable, outgoing, and enthusiastic. They love people. Actually, more like LOVE people. You'll most likely find them at social gatherings, trying to be the center of attention and entertaining the crowd. They are charming and usually full of energy and positive emotions (as they will gladly tell you).

Contrary to that, people scoring low on extroversion are more reserved, quiet, or withdrawn. They value their me-time and are much more introspective than their extroverted counterparts. Why waste your time and energy on other people when you can lose yourself in thoughts and daydreams?

The icon that best captures the essence of extroversion for me is the singer Lady Gaga (at least the public persona she portrays; I've sadly never met her). The eccentric singer is extremely outgoing and energetic. Her outfits are legendary. They are designed to attract as much attention as possible.

Agreeableness: The Mother Teresa trait

Agreeableness reflects people's need for cooperation and social harmony. It provides insights into the ways in which we express our opinions and manage relationships.

People scoring high on agreeableness are generally trusting, softhearted, generous, and sympathetic. Because they are all about social harmony, they avoid confrontation whenever possible, try their best to not offend or insult, and are prepared to make personal sacrifices in the service of others (e.g., through donations or volunteering).

In contrast, people scoring low on agreeableness are more competitive, stubborn, self-confident, or aggressive. They have no problem speaking up when they don't like something or when they believe something needs to be changed.

One of the agreeableness icons that has caught the public imagination is Mother Teresa, the selfless, generous, and caring nun who founded a religious congregation to help the most vulnerable members of society. A symbol for altruism and kindness. Her charity provided homes to patients dying of HIV/AIDS, leprosy, and tuberculosis, and today sponsors soup kitchens and mobile health clinics, and runs schools and orphanages.

Neuroticism: The Piglet trait

Finally, neuroticism (also known inversely as emotional stability) refers to the extent to which people experience negative emotions. It reflects the ease with which we cope with and respond to life's demands.

People scoring high on neuroticism are anxious, nervous, and moody. They tend to get irritated by seemingly small challenges and worry a lot. Am I going to get sick? Am I going to get fired? Is it safe to use the subway?

On the flip side, people scoring low on neuroticism are more emotionally stable, optimistic, and self-confident. They are generally easygoing and don't get stressed quickly. Missed the subway? Got a cryptic email from the boss? Having family over? Emotionally stable people keep calm and carry on.

The neuroticism icon is one of my favorite fictional characters: Piglet. Piglet is a young pig and one of Winnie the Pooh's best friends. In the Disney cartoon, he stutters, is constantly nervous, and fears the wind and darkness. When he gets scared, his ears start to twitch. Most of the time, Piglet thinks about all the possible ways in which situations could go wrong. His mind then races with negative thoughts that jump from one worst-case scenario to the next.

. . .

What defines who we are is our particular combination of these personality traits. It's what we call a personality profile.

Think back to Lady Gaga. I introduced her as the icon for extroversion, but she also scores high on openness. And these two characteristics aren't independent; they influence each other. It's unlikely, for example, that Lady Gaga would express her openness through shrill and unconventional outfits if she wasn't also extroverted and interested in attracting attention.

Imagine someone who is open-minded but rather introverted. Got someone? The friend that immediately comes to mind for me is a woman I went to grad school with. She was highly open-minded but also extremely introverted. As you can imagine, flashy clothes weren't exactly her thing. Instead, she loved going to the museum and devoured classic literature.

What's Your Personality?

Let's turn to you now. If you haven't taken a Big Five test before, I recommend investing the next few minutes doing so. It will make the rest of the book much more relevant and engaging. You can visit this book's official website, www.mindmasters.ai/mypersonality, or do a simpler paper-and-pencil version in appendix A at the end of the book.

As you respond to the questions and interpret your results, I want you to keep one thing in mind: there are no inherently good or bad traits. Scoring high or low on each of the five personality dimensions has its own unique advantages and disadvantages.

For example, you might be tempted to consider high agreeableness—the tendency to be trusting and caring—a good trait to have. Being friendly and trusting certainly has its advantages in some aspects of life (e.g., relationships and teamwork), but extreme levels of agreeableness can also be thought of as overly gullible, opportunistic, and lacking a necessary level of assertiveness.

Although being somewhat disagreeable (i.e., critical and competitive) might not make you a lot of friends, it is important when you have to make difficult decisions or take the lead in a competitive environment. The same is true for neuroticism. Few people want to be seen as anxious and vulnerable. However, while being highly neurotic certainly poses challenges for people's health, it is also often associated with great innovative potential and genius—especially when paired with high levels of openness. Just think of the founder of Apple, Steve Jobs. Known to be highly neurotic, Jobs's slightly eccentric nature and ability to be in touch with his own emotions is what made him one of the most successful figures of the twenty-first century.

Anyway, give it a go.

. . .

Now that you know how machines learn and what your own personality profile looks like, we are ready to dive into research on how computers can predict such profiles without you ever having to touch a questionnaire. I've already told you that computers are better than colleagues, friends, and family members when it comes to predicting your personality from Facebook likes. How do they do that? And what other pieces of the personality puzzle do our social media profiles hold?

2

The Identities We Craft Online

On December 17, 2020, thirteen-year-old P. Surya climbed on top of a train coach in New Delhi, India, to take a daring selfie. He touched a live wire and was burned alive. Surya's death is no isolated incident. Since 2011, more than 259 people around the world have died from selfie-related accidents. That's more deaths than caused by shark attacks. In India, the problem is so widespread that popular tourist destinations like Mumbai have instated selfie-free zones throughout the city. Similarly, the Russian government became so alarmed by the growing number of selfie-related deaths that it started to issue flyers educating the public on how to take safe selfies.

Why do people risk their lives hunting for the perfect Instagram picture or spend hours crafting the perfect TikTok video? Why are we so obsessed with sharing our lives on social media? The answer is simple: We are fighting for attention. We want to be seen.

As science has shown, self-disclosure is inherently rewarding. Sharing one's own opinion or attitudes with others causes a spike of activity in the brain's pleasure center.[1] That's the part of the brain that typically springs into action when we receive rewards such as food, money, sex, or heroin. Yes, you've read that correctly. Sharing information about yourself triggers a similar brain response to receiving money or having sex. In fact, it feels so good to talk about ourselves that we're willing to give up money to share our inner lives with others.

But that's only half the story. Social media platforms are designed to encourage self-disclosure by making sharing easy and socially rewarding. How often do you check your likes, shares, or retweets? Every thirty minutes? Every ten? Every five? As social beings, we crave positive feedback from our environment and those around us. This feedback functionality is what makes social media sites so addictive.

It's also what makes social media sites the ideal hunting ground for what psychologists refer to as *identity claims*—deliberate expressions of a person's identity. Just as I communicated my identity to the other people in my village by putting a provoking bumper sticker on my car, dying my hair, or wearing a Ramones sweatshirt, social media platforms encourage their users to tell their stories and share their identities with others. You might follow Beyoncé's official fan page, post about your vacation to the Seychelles, or share a picture of the delicious burger you've had for lunch. A staggering 80 percent of the status updates posted on social media sites such as Facebook or X/Twitter are directly focused on a person's immediate experience.[2]

We naturally assume that these traces hold information about their owners. Why otherwise would recruiters consult applicants' social media pages before hiring? Why would the US government encourage visa applicants to link their social media accounts? And why would most of us stalk our dates online before meeting them?

Research confirms our intuition. By studying the social media profiles of strangers, we can gain valid insights into their psychology.[3] But our judgments aren't nearly as accurate as those made by computers.

The ABCs of Algorithmic Snooping

The intuition behind psychological targeting is simple. Imagine you are part of a profiling unit at the FBI. You've been given the following profile: Target X, an anonymous user who likes Hello Kitty, posts about their passion for anime and manga characters, and shares videos of the famous Korean band BTS.

Now describe the user to me. Make an educated guess of who they are. Their age, gender, ethnicity, and personality. Here's my best guess: Teenage girl. Asian. Introverted and open-minded, possibly neurotic. I assume your guess might have looked similar (there is typically a high level of consensus).

How did you arrive at your conclusion? You most likely drew on your experience. Your recollection and impression of people with similar interests to the mysterious Target X. This could be people you are close to. People you know tangentially through friends. Or people you've only seen on TV. When we judge strangers based on our observations of their behavior, we tend to think of the prototypical person of the same behavioral profile—the mode (i.e., most common option) or average, if you want.

In the absence of any other information, taking the average person as your comparison point is your best bet (and the computer's, too). You will, of course, make mistakes. It turns out that the Guinness World Record for the largest collection of Hello Kitty memorabilia in 2017 was held by sixty-seven-year-old Masao Gunji, a retired police officer from Japan.[4]

The predictions we make—and the relationships these predictions are based on—are probabilistic, not deterministic. They help us make educated guesses about the world with incomplete information. It's far more likely that the Target X profile belongs to a young teenage girl than a sixty-seven-year-old retired police officer. But we should never use our intuitions to jump to definitive conclusions about any one individual.

The same is true for the predictions computers make. Their predictions might be more systematic than ours, but they always reflect educated guesses, never the truth. An algorithm's judgment of a person's characteristics are overgeneralizations and can therefore seem rather stereotypical.

Look at the word clouds in figure 2-1, which were published in a paper by Andrew Schwartz and colleagues in 2013. They show the words in people's Facebook status updates that are most indicative of being male or female (top = female, bottom = male), broken down into a general word cloud in the middle as well as clustered topics on the outer rim. (You can classify people's gender with an accuracy of over 90 percent just by looking at what they post on social media.) The bigger the word, the more strongly it is correlated with being male or female; and the darker the word, the more often it appears in people's statuses. (You can scan the QR code on your phone or tablet to see the word clouds in color.)

The word clouds are just as stereotypical as my Target X example but based on actual data. Women post about shopping, babies, and boyfriends, while men swear and chat about sports and video games. Perhaps women really are from Venus and men from Mars after all.

As we dive into the science of psychological targeting together, it is important to remember that the relationships I'm going to show you are free of any normative judgment. They describe the world as it is (or was, as we typically work with historical data), not how it ought to be—a critical distinction between description and prescription that I will highlight repeatedly throughout the first part of the book.

It is also important to remember that the insights aren't limited to specific platforms. Much of my own research—and that of my colleagues—has relied on Facebook data. But you can make similar predictions with data from all the other social platforms like TikTok, Instagram, Reddit, Snapchat, and more. Whenever there's a way for people to express themselves online, there's a way to gather identity claims and turn them into psychological profiles.

The World of Facebook Likes

The Facebook Like (aka: thumbs up) is an iconic feature of the platform. It's an easy way for users to express what they care about and

FIGURE 2-1

Words in users' Facebook status updates indicating gender

Female

Male

Scan the QR code for a color version of the word clouds.

Source: H. Andrew Schwartz et al., "Personality, Gender, and Age in the Language of Social Media: The Open-Vocabulary Approach," *PloS One* 8, no. 9 (2013): e73791, https://doi.org/10.1371/journal.pone .0073791. Permission via https://creativecommons.org/licenses/by/4.0/.

to appreciate the content that other users generate and share. We've all been there. Friend 1 posts a cute cat video and we like it. Then Friend 2 posts a snarky comment making fun of Friend 1 for posting cat videos—and we like that, too. A fun pastime, for sure.

But these aren't the kind of likes I am going to discuss in this chapter. I focus on the official Facebook pages users can like or follow. The official Facebook page of soccer player Lionel Messi has around 101 million followers, for example. Taylor Swift has 77 million, and Barack Obama, 56 million. But it's not just celebrities and other big shots that have Facebook pages. Anyone can create one. In 2019, there were over 60 million active Facebook pages.

Why Facebook pages? In 2013, together with two of his colleagues, Michal Kosinski showed that Facebook likes were predictive of a whole range of sociodemographic and psychological characteristics: people's age, gender, drug use, political ideology, sexual orientation, IQ, life satisfaction, and personality.[5] In addition to reporting the accuracy of their predictive models, their paper also included a host of examples of Facebook pages that are indicative of different personal traits.

Look at the two lists of Facebook likes in table 2-1. They are both related to the personality trait of extroversion. One of them reflects people who are reserved and quiet (introverted), and the other reflects people who are outgoing and social (extroverted). I want you to guess which list is which.

Got your answer? Let's see. Extroverts are on the left, introverts on the right. If you happen to like beer pong (a popular party game in which players try to land a Ping-Pong ball in a cup of beer across the table), cheerleading, or Michael Jordan (list A), you are more likely to be extroverted. If, instead, you are more interested in anime, Minecraft, or Terry Pratchett (list B), you are more likely to be introverted.

Makes a lot of sense, no? Extroverts are energetic, talkative, and sociable, making it hardly surprising that the majority of extroverted likes are related to social activities (e.g., beer pong, cheerleading, dancing, socializing) and have a certain degree of attention-seeking potential (e.g., cheerleading, modeling, dancing).

TABLE 2-1

Facebook likes related to the personality trait of extroversion

List A	List B
Beer pong	RPGs
Michael Jordan	Fanfiction.net
Dancing	Programming
Socializing	Anime
Chris Tucker	Manga
I feel better tan	Video games
Modeling	Role-playing games
Cheerleading	Minecraft
Theater	Voltaire
Flip cup	Terry Pratchett

Source: Adapted from Michal Kosinski, David Stillwell, and Thore Graepel, "Private Traits and Attributes Are Predictable from Digital Records of Human Behavior," *Proceedings of the National Academy of Sciences* 110, no. 15 (2013): 5802–5805.

The same degree of intuitiveness applies to the list of introverted likes. Knowing that introverts are typically shy, reserved, and quiet, it makes sense that they would favor activities that don't require other people (e.g., programming, reading anime or Terry Pratchett novels, and playing video games).

Let's look at another example. This time I will let you try to guess which personality trait is associated with the two lists in table 2-2. Remember, we still have openness, conscientiousness, agreeableness, and neuroticism in the race (feel free to skip back to the summary of all the personality traits in table 1-1 if you want).

What do circles of prayer, *Redeeming Love*, and Compassion International have in common? And how do they differ from I hate everyone, you, and police, and Julius Caesar? The first list leaves you with this warm glow, while the second list generates a considerable amount

TABLE 2-2

List of Facebook likes related to one of the Big Five personality traits

Continue reading to see which one.

List A	List B
Compassion International	I hate everyone
Logan Utah	I hate you
Jon Foreman	I hate police
Redeeming Love	Friedrich Nietzsche
Pornography harms	Timmy from South Park
The Book of Mormon	Atheism/Satanism
Circles of prayer	Prada
Go to church	Sun Tzu
Christianity	Julius Caesar
Marianne Williamson	Knives

Source: Adapted from Michal Kosinski, David Stillwell, and Thore Graepel, "Private Traits and Attributes Are Predictable from Digital Records of Human Behavior," *Proceedings of the National Academy of Sciences* 110, no. 15 (2013): 5802–5805.

of discomfort. Settled on a personality trait? It's agreeableness (the lists for the three remaining personality traits are in appendix B).

List A speaks to people who are caring, trusting, and empathetic—the nice guys who are embedded in their church community and give to charity. List B is the opposite. A bunch of critical and competitive people who hate pretty much everything, are into knives and Satanism, and follow role models such as Julius Caesar, Sun Tzu, and Timmy from South Park. And it's finally confirmed by science: the devil does wear Prada!

Here's a bonus round. Table 2-3 shows a psychological characteristic that you all know (I promise), but not it's not a personality trait. Take a look at the two lists and see if you can figure it out.

TABLE 2-3

List of Facebook likes related to a psychological characteristic

Continue reading to see which one.

List A	List B
The Godfather	Jason Aldean
Mozart	Tyler Perry
Thunderstorms	Sephora
The Colbert Report	CHiQ
Morgan Freeman's voice	Bret Michaels
The Daily Show	Clark Griswold
Lord of the Rings	Bebe
To Kill a Mockingbird	I love being a mom
Science	Harley Davidson
Curly fries	Lady Antebellum

Source: Adapted from Michal Kosinski, David Stillwell, and Thore Graepel, "Private Traits and Attributes Are Predictable from Digital Records of Human Behavior," *Proceedings of the National Academy of Sciences* 110, no. 15 (2013): 5802–5805.

I'm going to give you a hint. You will probably find it easier to guess the trait if you focus on list A. The likes I would consider most intuitive are science, *To Kill a Mockingbird*, and Mozart.

The answer is intelligence (or what we today call *cognitive ability*). List A reflects high intelligence; list B, low intelligence. As you can see, list A relates to reading, sophisticated humor, and science. In contrast, the items on list B are a lot more down-to-earth and tangible.

The only question mark is curly fries. Why on earth would liking curly fries—as delicious as they are—be related to high intelligence? There is no obvious reason. Yet, they were in the data Kosinski and his colleagues studied. It's possible that there was a group of highly intelligent college students who all decided to like curly fries. Or perhaps there is logic to it, and I am just not intelligent enough to figure it out. It could be all the above, or none. We simply don't know.

The reason I bring up this example is because it illustrates an important lesson regarding the relationships between our digital footprints and psychological characteristics. The relationships we observe are not causal. Eating curly fries will not make you more intelligent, and it's equally unlikely that being more intelligent makes you genetically predisposed to liking curly fries. But just because we cannot explain the relationship between the two doesn't mean we cannot use it. Void of any understanding, the relationship can still help us make predictions.

If my goal is to predict whether a person is intelligent, I might not care about the deeper meaning of the cues. It doesn't really matter if I understand why liking curly fries is related to higher intelligence. All that matters is that it is. If I trust the data, I should assume that the next person I meet who likes curly fries on Facebook is also relatively intelligent.

To be clear, the relationship between liking curly fries and intelligence might change over time (and the fact that there's no obvious reason for it to exist in the first place makes this much more likely). But at least in the moment you observe a particular relationship, this relationship will help you predict your outcome regardless of whether you understand its meaning or not.

The World of Words

Take a look at the two X/Twitter posts and try to conjure an image of the two authors. What do they look like? How old are they? Are they more likely to be female or male? Outgoing or shy? Liberal or conservative?

GOODBYE COVID HELLO DANCING 🍵 💕 happy for Australia! Praying for the rest of the world that we can all be dancing together soon ⛪

On #MLKDay 🗿, we celebrate his life but we're also called
to live out his values through service of our own. Here are
some ways you can get involved in your community:

The first tweet comes from Lady Gaga; the second from Barack
Obama. You might not have thought of Lady Gaga and Barack Obama
when reading those tweets, but I bet that the images you created in
your mind were probably not too far off.

The psychologist James Pennebaker at the University of Texas at
Austin was among the first to advocate for the power of language as
a window into our psyche. Pennebaker studied how writing about our
traumatic experiences could help us heal.[6]

While reading through some of the essays his patients had written, he couldn't help but notice how different the essays were, in both
content and style. While some people recited their trauma almost in
a matter-of-fact tone without revealing any emotional identification
with the story, others seemed to be consumed by anger and despair.
Yet others reflected on what had happened with an optimistic out-
look on the future.

Could these differences predict how well an individual might cope
with their trauma? Could they be used to learn something about the
inner mental states of these individuals?

In his quest to answer these questions, Pennebaker created an
entire field of scientific inquiry based on the idea that one can objec-
tively quantify aspects of language and relate them to our psychological experiences (I will return to Pennebaker and his findings later,
so stay tuned).

What makes language such a fascinating puzzle piece of who we
are is that it is ubiquitous. We spend about 50–80 percent of our waking hours engaged in some kind of communication. This could mean
greeting a stranger in the subway, engaging in a deep conversation
with one of our close friends, writing an email to a colleague, leaving
a voice message for our children, or noting down our thoughts in a
diary. But it could also mean posting on our social media platform of
(experimental) choice: Facebook.

The word clouds in figure 2-2 were generated based on the Facebook status updates of almost seventy-five thousand users. If you're old enough, young enough, or simply self-disciplined enough to not have a Facebook account, let me bring you up to speed on what Facebook status updates are (and convey my admiration; well done!). Facebook status updates give users the chance to share what's on their mind through text, images, or videos. You can decide to share the content within your circle of friends only or distribute it publicly for the entire world to see.

All you need to create these word clouds—and unlock the psychological secrets of language—is simply count how often different words appear in the status update of a particular user. How often does the person talk about parties, the weekend, or computers? Once you have done this for all the seventy-five thousand users in your dataset, you can start connecting the dots by calculating basic correlations between relative word frequencies and personality traits. It's that easy.

Now take a closer look at the two word clouds (as before, the bigger the word, the more strongly it is associated with the respective personality trait; the darker the word, the more common it is). Any ideas which personality trait they might represent? It's extroversion, again (A = extroversion, B = introversion). You can literally see the introverted geek sitting in front of their computer, browsing the internet, just having finished reading another anime comic. And you can conjure an image of the outgoing extrovert who is sooooo excited about the amazing night out planned for next weekend. Gotta love the girlz! I might have been able to predict that extroverts talk about parties. But I would have never thought to put the words "sooooooo" or "gotta" on my list of indicators. That's an insight that only the data itself could offer me.

Figure 2-3 is my personal favorite (the remaining three personality traits are in appendix B). The figure shows only the first half. It's high agreeableness. The word cloud has this warm glow to it. It is full of praise, blessed thank-you notes, merry Thanksgiving and Christmas celebrations, and an overwhelming feeling that the world is just a

FIGURE 2-2

The words in people's Facebook status updates most strongly correlated with being extroverted and introverted

Scan the QR code for a color version of the word clouds.

FIGURE 2-3

The words in people's Facebook status updates most strongly correlated with agreeableness

Scan the QR code for a color version
of the word cloud.

Source: H. Andrew Schwartz et al., "Personality, Gender, and Age in the Language of Social Media: The Open-Vocabulary Approach," *PloS One* 8, no. 9 (2013): e73791, https://doi.org/10.1371/journal.pone.0073791. Permission via https://creativecommons.org/licenses/by/4.0/.

wonderful place. Before you look at the word cloud for low agreeableness, guess what it might look like. Which words could be indicative of having a rather critical, competitive, and quarrelsome personality? Got a mental image in your mind? A word of warning: it's not going to be pretty. You can see it in figure 2-4.

No additional commentary needed.

But personality isn't the only psychological characteristic we can infer from language. I already mentioned the work by psychologist James Pennebaker, who started studying the links between language and mental health in the 1980s and 1990s. About three decades—and many methodological advances—later, we have ample evidence that

FIGURE 2-4

The words in people's Facebook status updates most strongly correlated with low agreeableness

Scan the QR code for a color version of the word cloud.

Source: H. Andrew Schwartz et al., "Personality, Gender, and Age in the Language of Social Media: The Open-Vocabulary Approach," *PloS One* 8, no. 9 (2013): e73791, https://doi.org/10.1371/journal.pone.0073791. Permission via https://creativecommons.org/licenses/by/4.0/.

Pennebaker's intuition was spot on: our language offers a glimpse into our psychological well-being and mental health.

Take the use of first-person pronouns such as "I," "me," or "myself," for example. Any thoughts on what using these words might say about you? My first guess when Pennebaker asked this question at an academic conference was that it had to be narcissism. "Why would anyone care about anything other than me? Come on folks, pay attention to who's really important here!" I was wrong. References to yourself don't make you a narcissist. Instead, they are indicators of emotional distress.

Surprised? So was I. But take a moment and think back to the last time you felt really down. What were you thinking about? The future of humanity? Unlikely! When we feel down, we typically think of ourselves. Why am I feeling so bad? Am I ever going to get better? Why can't I deal with this situation more successfully? When things look dreary for us, we tend to look inward, focus on ourselves, and ruminate.

And because we cannot constantly monitor our thoughts and feelings (especially when we are feeling down), this inner monologue creeps into the language we use when expressing ourselves to others. We might not openly admit to feeling blue, but we can't help talking more about ourselves than usual. A study by Allison Tackman and colleagues from the University of Arizona suggests that individuals suffering from depression use about 40 percent more first-person pronouns than their healthy counterparts; that's six hundred a day.[7]

But it's not just the extent to which we talk about ourselves that gives away how we feel. One of my favorite studies in this space was conducted by the psychologist Johannes Eichstaedt and colleagues, who examined the Facebook status updates and medical records of 683 patients.[8] Just by looking at the words people used to describe their experiences on Facebook, Eichstaedt could accurately predict whether a person was suffering from depression in 72 percent of the cases (with 50 percent being chance, or a coin flip).

Seventy-two percent might seem far from perfect. It is. Ideally you want that number to be as close to 100 percent as possible. However, it turns out that 72 percent is about as good as the accuracy of short screening surveys that are commonly used in a mental health diagnostic. And suddenly a 72 percent accuracy achieved by a computer model snooping through your Facebook statuses becomes rather remarkable.

Let's explore some of the relationships underlying these predictions. The word clouds in figure 2-5 show the words (organized by topics) that are most indicative of being depressed. They relate to negative mood and affect (tears, crying, feeling sick), interpersonal

FIGURE 2-5

The words in people's Facebook status updates most strongly correlated with clinical depression

Depressed mood and feeling

Loneliness   ### Hostility

Somatic complaints   ### Medical references

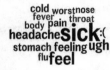 

Scan the QR code for a color version of the word clouds.

Source: Johannes C. Eichstaedt, et al., "Facebook Language Predicts Depression in Medical Records," *Proceedings of the National Academy of Sciences* 115, no. 44 (2018): 11203–11208.

challenges including loneliness and hostility (miss, irked, upset, nerves, hate), and somatic complaints with medical references (headache, sick, hurt, pain, hospital).

As I said before, we cannot make any claims about cause and effect. Does being lonely cause people to be depressed or is loneliness a by-product of depression? Does experiencing somatic health problems result in mental health issues, or is poor mental health contributing to physical symptoms? Most likely, the links cut both ways. But this doesn't matter if your goal is to simply identify people at risk (and ideally offer them support).

What I find particularly fascinating about these word clouds is the strong connection between physical health (i.e., somatic complaints) and mental health. We often think of the body and the mind in isolation. Yet, Eichstaedt's research suggests that both are intricately linked. Physical pain can easily turn into a mental one, and vice versa. As these findings highlight, linking digital footprints to psychological traits does not only open a window into people's psychology but can also teach us invaluable insights into our collective psychology.

Sometimes these insights are entertaining. Sometimes they are reassuring. And sometimes they are rather disturbing. Let me show you what I mean by this with a final example. It's not a psychological trait in the classic sense. Yet, it's a personal characteristic that most of us consider private: our income or socioeconomic standing.

Less than 10 percent of users on online dating platforms provide information about their income, and most people do not discuss their salaries even with their closest friends or family members. Although the National Labor Relations Act of 1935 granted employees in the United States the right to disclose their salaries, the cultural norm still considers it inappropriate. A commentator in *The Atlantic* skillfully captured this sentiment in his comparison: "Asking a coworker about pay seems akin to asking about their sex life."[9]

As some of my own research has shown, a relatively simple model trained on people's Facebook status updates can guess an individual's income with a margin of error of about $10,000.[10] Not perfect, but not bad either. However, what really struck me were some of the relationships we observed in the data. Look at the word clouds in figure 2-6. The differences in what the wealthy and the poor talk about are remarkable and paint a disturbing—yet not necessarily unexpected—picture.

High-income individuals talk about vacations (e.g., vacation, flight, beach, Vegas, airport) and pleasant activities that usually require

FIGURE 2-6

The words in people's Facebook status updates most strongly correlated with level of income

High

Low

Scan the QR code for a color version of the word clouds.

Source: Sandra C. Matz, et al., "Predicting Individual-Level Income from Facebook Profiles," *PloS One* 14, no. 3 (2019): e0214369, https://doi.org/10.1371/journal.pone.0214369.

spending a considerable amount of money (e.g., shopping, celebrating). They express positive emotions (e.g., excited to, great) and use future-oriented words and phrases (e.g., looking forward to, afterwards). Low-income individuals, on the other hand, are more self-focused (e.g., I need, I can, I got, me), express themselves through more colloquial language (e.g., idk, cuz), share predominantly negative feelings (e.g., hurt, hate, bored), and use more swear words and emoticons.

If you find these word clouds troubling, you are not alone. They are. But as much as I would like them to be different, they are not. That's what the world looks like when you are poor.

The ability to reflect uncomfortable truths back at us is part of what makes big data powerful. It offers a window into the lives of others, providing us with perspectives that we might otherwise not have access to. In some instances, these insights are hilarious (think back to the word clouds for agreeableness). In other instances, the results might be shocking and condemning of the societies we live in. But having access to this descriptive reality is an opportunity to point out pressing social issues, and to garner support for change.

It is not surprising, for example, that low-income individuals are more self-focused, while their high-income counterparts dream about the future. It's not that poor people are selfish. It's that thinking about the future is pretty damn hard when you are struggling to make ends meet in the now. It's a luxury to not have to think about yourself and the precarious financial situation you might be in all the time.

The World of Pixels

We all know the adage "A picture is worth a thousand words." This certainly feels true when it comes to seeing your niece sprout her first tooth or take her first bike ride. You might get a sense of what's happening if your brother or sister describes this experience in an email or text message. But it's not the same as receiving a picture or, even better, a video of the event. The experience becomes so much more relatable and real.

But is this also true in the world of psychological targeting? Are the pictures we post more predictive of who we are than the words we speak? The short answer is no. Based on the latest science, pictures are less predictive of psychological traits than Facebook likes or language. However, that doesn't mean they don't offer any insights (and could very well change in the future when we have more sophisticated ways to analyze them). A computer trying to distinguish between an extrovert and an introvert, for example, will be right in about 70 percent of cases (50 percent is chance). If you were to attempt the same task, you'd be right only about 60 percent of the time.

Turning pictures into psychological profiles isn't a trivial task. Pictures are a nightmare to work with. They are unstructured and complex. Facebook likes are straightforward to quantify. You either like a page or you don't. It's a one or a zero. Easy enough. Words are a tad more complicated but still easy to count. Pictures, on the other hand, are a combination of millions of pixels that only make sense when you put them together a certain way.

The simplest way of analyzing pictures is to break down their complexity into a finite set of concrete features. For example, you might start by identifying the objects that are present in your picture. A chair, multiple people, a cat, glasses, a lamp. No need to do this manually; object recognition algorithms will do the job for you. What else? You can describe the image's color. Lots of red, a bit of blue. High saturation, mostly warm colors. From there, you could jump to the image's composition (if you are a photographer, you know what I'm talking about). How are the elements of the image organized? Is it broken down into many small distinct regions, or does it mostly consist of a few larger ones? Are the elements symmetrical? This is just to give you an idea. There's almost no limit to how many features you can extract.

Let's have a look at an example from the work of the Italian computer scientist Cristina Segalin, who has shown that the pictures we post and like on social media are about as predictive of our personality as our credit card spending (which I will get to in the next chapter).[11] The two collages you'll see when scanning the following QR code (sorry, that's your only option as we need color for this one) show Flickr pictures that people added to their list of favorites (Flickr used to be a leading image and video hosting platform with social network features; it's still around, but far less popular than it used to be). If you cannot access the pictures, let me describe them to you. One is a happy mix of colorful images featuring flowers, sunsets, cultural sites, and food. The other one is a rather gloomy assembly of mostly gray images without a particular topical focus. Any guesses which personality trait the two collages might reflect? It's neuroticism.

You might be asking yourself: Is it really so surprising (or interesting) that the pictures people like or post tell us something about who they are? Isn't that the whole point of liking and posting them in the first place?! And the clues the algorithm uses to make predictions of people's personality don't seem to be about the person either. It's the colors and basic content of the picture that drive the judgments. Fair point. Up to now, that was the case. But it's not the only signal computers can use to snoop around your inner mental life.

I Can See It on Your Face

The part I have left out so far is the most contested among scientists and usually makes people recoil (including myself). But it's also the part that—if true—should give you pause and make you reconsider the way you think about photographs. I'm talking about the ability to predict people's psychological characteristics from their faces.

Physiognomy—the art of judging someone's character from facial characteristics—isn't new. It has a long and dark history that reaches all the way back to ancient Greece. Pythagoras is said to have selected his students based on their facial features. The captain of the *Beagle* almost canceled Charles Darwin's historic voyage because he thought Darwin's nose revealed a lack of determination and energy. Cesare Lombroso (the founding father of criminal anthropology) believed that criminals could be identified by features such as the softness of their skin, a childlike appearance, or the thickness of their hair. And lead scientists in the Nazi regime used pseudoscientific evidence to perpetuate anti-Semitism.

Eventually, the validity of such physiognomic claims was universally debunked. The idea that one could infer personal characteristics from people's physical appearance, especially their face, fell out of fashion. Rightfully so. None of the original claims made by the early advocates of physiognomy could stand the test of solid scientific inquiry, and many of the use cases were horrific.

However, recent advances in computer vision have rekindled the scientific interest in the relationships between our physical features and our personality and character. That brings me back to an old friend of ours, Michal Kosinski (yes, he likes controversial topics), whose research suggests that computers can accurately predict your personality, sexual orientation, and even political ideology from your face.

Take one of the most controversial findings, for example: the ability of computers to predict whether you identify as straight or gay just by observing your face.[12] With only one picture, the computer's accuracy for male targets is 81 percent. With five pictures, that accuracy shoots up to 91 percent. For women, the accuracies are slightly lower, with 71 percent for one picture and 83 percent for five.

If what I've just said makes you uneasy and question whether I might be delusional, I get it. The thought that my personality, sexual orientation, or political ideology could be predicted just by looking at my face is spooky to say the least. It's also hard to believe that it could be true. When I first heard about the research, I thought it was ridiculous. I wasn't alone in this sentiment. The work of Kosinski and others has received substantial pushback, both from the public and from other researchers.

But bear with me for a minute and let me channel Kosinski's arguments for why we might, in principle, expect our faces to be reflective of our inner mental lives. Let's start with a source that is utterly unscientific: the lyrics of the 1972 song "The Story of Your Life Is in Your Face" by the American singer-songwriter Tom Hall:

> *He said the story of your life is in your face*
> *It's written there in little subtle lines*
> *The story of your life is in your face*
> *What's written on your face has been heavy on your mind*

The song is a beautiful homage to how our faces act as a canvas for our emotions. Smile lines, for example, tell the tales of a life filled with happiness and laughter—both of which are known to be the hallmark of extroversion. As our psychological experiences accumulate over the years, they might alter our physical appearance, including our facial features.

Similarly, it's likely that our facial features exercise at least some influence over our character. Say you are born a beautiful baby. Symmetric face, big eyes, rosy cheeks. Like it or not, Mother Nature has set you up for success. As a toddler, adults might stop more often to say hi and smile at you. As a teenager, you might be more popular. Would it really be so surprising that with all these positive social experiences, you might turn out a little bit more extroverted? This isn't just a hypothetical example but an actual scientific finding. Attractive individuals receive more positive social feedback from their environment and as a result become more extroverted.[13]

And finally, there is a whole list of factors that could influence both facial features and psychological characteristics. Think of your upbringing, environmental factors, or simply variations in hormone levels.

Take testosterone, for example, which naturally occurs in all of us. What do you associate with this hormone? Masculinity? Aggression? Risk-taking? Well, all of them are true. Testosterone levels influence your physical appearance by making you look more masculine (e.g., impacting the width-to-height ratio of your face). At the same time, giving people testosterone can alter their behavior and personality such that they become more aggressive and risk-seeking.

Let's say the history of physiognomics didn't exist, and I had just told you about all the possible pathways by which facial features and personal characteristics might be related. Don't you think there is at least some reason to consider it a possibility?

To be clear, this isn't necessarily great news. If we can predict a person's traits from their face, that could have terrible consequences (as Kosinski himself warns in his work). But how we feel about the implications of such research should be independent of whether we believe the research itself.

Into the Deep

With that in mind, let's start exploring how algorithms can use your face as a window into what lies beyond. As we've seen before, computers can extract a list of features related to a picture's content, color, composition, and so on. Faces are different. Two eyes, one mouth, and a nose. Not exactly master snooping material. We need more information. Real magic. The closest we can get to this is a computational approach called deep learning or deep neural networks.

Deep learning is an attempt at getting computers to mimic how the human brain works. As humans, we look at an object or scene and immediately know what's going on. We process the millions of light particles that hit our retina every millisecond and weave them into a coherent image. What's going on behind the scenes are billions of neurons firing at different levels of cognitive abstraction.

Deep learning is based on the same idea. Just like the human brain, deep neural networks consist of several layers of neurons that process information and decide whether to pass on this information to the next layer. Instead of working with a predetermined set of features, neural networks start by considering every single pixel in an image (lowest layer). Over many (many!) trial-and-error runs, the networks learn how certain constellations of pixels are related to more abstract concepts (e.g., does this picture contain a cat or is this face extroverted?).

You can think of it as an organization. There are different levels of hierarchy, with many workers at the bottom and a CEO at the top. At each level of the organization, employees must process information and decide what their superiors need to know. This goes all the way up to the top. While the CEO never sees all the individual pieces of information, their decisions are (ideally) informed by the collective knowledge of the organization.

The computational models themselves are too complex to interpret. But we don't need to understand the model's neural architecture to get a sense of what's going on under the hood. If a model can accurately classify people into extroverts and introverts (based on our validation against self-reported survey responses), then the model must be doing something right. Which means that we can simply scrutinize the predictions it makes.

Take a look at the two photos in figure 2-7. They are taken from ongoing work by Michal Kosinski and Poruz Khambatta.

I know. They look like dreamy, soft-focus portraits. And they kind of are. These are depictions of an introvert and extrovert, as dreamed up by an algorithm. One photo is the combination (a morph) of the female faces in the dataset that were predicted to be most extroverted, and the other is a combination of the ones that were predicted to be most introverted (and yes, you can do the same thing for men and ethnicities other than Caucasian; you just can't mix them).

I'm sure you have a sense which one is which. Introverts are on the left; extroverts are on the right. How did you arrive at that conclusion? The eyes? The hair? The shape of the face?

FIGURE 2-7

Morphs of the ten most introverted and extroverted faces as predicted by the algorithm

Scan the QR code for a color version of the photos.

Source: Michal Kosinski, "The End of Privacy," paper presented at the annual convention of the Society for Personality and Social Psychology, San Diego, January 28–30, 2016.

Here's what I see when I look at the pictures: the faces of extroverts are slimmer, they smile, their eyes appear to be bigger and lighter colored, they don't have outlines of glasses, and they have lighter hair (I recommend scanning the QR code to see the color version; the differences are much more striking there).

And here's what I intuit from my observations: Extroverted women are vain; they dye their hair, refuse to wear glasses, and swap out the boring transparent contact lenses for blue ones. What about their faces being slimmer? Well, it could be that extroverts are more obsessed with their weight. But it could also be that they are simply better at taking pictures. They might have figured out that taking photos from above makes your face look slimmer. I'm sure introverts figured that out as well. But they might simply not care. Want more evidence for this theory? Check out the nostrils. Clearly visible for introverts but not at all visible for extroverts.

This raises an important question. How much of what the algorithm picks up on are actual differences in facial features as opposed to grooming habits and the ways in which people take pictures? If all you care about is accurately predicting people's personality traits, this distinction might not bother you all that much. If the signal is consistent, you might take all the grooming cues you can get.

However, if you are a scientist claiming direct relationships between facial features and personal characteristics, you need a better answer. Kosinski and Khambatta were well aware of this.

So, their team invited students at Stanford University to their lab. All participants were asked to come shaved, without makeup, and with their hair pulled back with a hair band. All pictures were taken from exactly the same angle, using the same background, and the same camera. In other words, the pictures were held as constant and free of confounding signals as possible. If the effects from the two online samples were a mere artifact of grooming and photography skills, Kosinski's algorithm should fail spectacularly in this highly controlled sample. It didn't. It did just as well as in the original sample (or even better).

Beyond Social Media

As a computational social scientist, I am fascinated by the ability of computers to turn social media profiles into highly intimate predictions of people's psychology. It's remarkable. Groundbreaking.

However, as a social media user myself, the idea is far less appealing. It's creepy. Intrusive. If you are one of the lucky few who resisted the social media vortex or deleted your account for good, you might be patting yourself on the shoulder right now. Well done, you saved yourself from the evil grip of Big Brother, while the rest of us are doomed. I wish that was true. But it's not.

Just think back to the power of words when it comes to revealing a person's inner mental state. Sure, you can get those words from social media. It's an easy starting point. But we don't have to rely on written language posted on social media to make inferences about who you are. Advances in speech-recognition technology have made it easier than ever before to transcribe spoken words to written language. What used to take hours of manual transcription can now be done in seconds at the ease of a click. Instead of relying on your social media posts, we can simply eavesdrop on your conversations. You probably have a smartphone, don't you? And maybe other smart devices such as Alexa or a Samsung TV that come equipped with voice control.

The same is true for pictures. They have a property that makes them particularly challenging when it comes to privacy. Any ideas? If nothing comes to mind, you are probably thinking of your own pictures. There's nothing inherently wrong with sharing those on social media. It can feel good to have others share the moments that matter to us. But that's only a small portion of the pictures of us circulating out there.

Your friends might post pictures of your latest weekend trip to the Hamptons, and your colleague might share that selfie you took at the holiday party. Or you might just happen to walk past in the background of the TikTok video of a complete stranger during their Bahamas vacation. To let you in on the fun, your friends will probably tag you. And even if they don't, facial recognition algorithms can take over that job in a matter of seconds. While you have control over the pages you follow or the things you post about, pictures often have a life of their own. And last time I checked, there was no way to simply leave your face at home if you wanted to go unnoticed.

More importantly, social media isn't the only snapshot of your digital life. There are many other data sources that don't require curated input or even your direct cooperation to keep track of your behavior. Your Google searches create a log of your most intimate secrets and questions. Your credit card knows exactly what, where, and when you buy. And your smartphone is equipped with an army of sensors that collect your current location, screen for ambient light, capture physical activity, and gauge how many social interactions you have (e.g., by monitoring your calls and messages).

Resisting the temptation of using social media might be great for your well-being. But it will not protect you from leaving the types of digital traces that can be used to profile your psychology. As I will show you in the next chapter, you can and will be seen.

3

The Digital Breadcrumbs
of Our Existence

I was standing next to the stage of a small auditorium at the W Hotel in Chicago, waiting to deliver a talk on the science of happiness. With just a few moments to go, my heart started to beat faster. I was nervous—the type of nervous that makes you question your life choices.

Why had I agreed to this? What did I (or anyone for that matter) know about the topic of digital happiness? Was that even a thing or just a made-up item on a corporate bullshit bingo list? But it was too late for second guesses. Everything was ready. I was mic'd up, my first slide was showing on the screen, and the moderator was about to introduce me to the crowd.

That's when one of the organizers pulled me aside.

The second speaker for the session hadn't shown up. The organizer had tried to call him multiple times, but no answer. Would I be willing to speak for an entire hour instead of thirty minutes? Ah . . . a bit of a surprise, but sure.

I was on fire. My audience was engaged, my jokes were landing, and I had extra time for additional anecdotes and insights. In short, I was crushing it.

But about twenty-five minutes into my talk, the organizers signaled to me that the other speaker had arrived. I had to wrap up within the next five to ten minutes.

Seriously? What a jerk! Shows up late and steals my extra time. I hope he sucks.

I wrapped up hastily—smiling on the outside but boiling on the inside—and walked off the stage.

Fast-forward six hours. After a dinner reception with the conference attendees, I find myself sitting in a bar with . . . well, yes, "the other speaker." He's hot, smart, and funny. We have a few cocktails, play Ping-Pong (I'm not holding back; this is not a friendly match), and gossip about other academics we know. When the bar closes, it doesn't take much convincing to get me to come back to his place.

As soon as we enter his apartment, I start snooping around. I want to gauge his character. For all I know he could be a hot, smart, and funny serial killer.

The first thing I notice is a huge library wall filled with books. Books in English, French, and Hebrew about science, literature, and art. They're sorted according to topic and height, all perfectly aligned with the front edge of the shelves. Who is this person? An organized bookworm? Borderline obsessive-compulsive?

Next: drinks. I open the cabinets to look for glasses. They are all perfectly spaced and sparkling clean. Not a single watermark. I wonder if that's his magic or his cleaner's? I get my answer when I return to the living room and attempt to put our drinks down on the coffee table. He jumps up from his chair to place coasters underneath the glasses. Borderline obsessive-compulsive, indeed.

The night went well. Very well. Fast-forward another four years. The mysterious bookworm and I are exchanging rings in a small loft in Manhattan, saying *yes* to a lifetime together.

The first impressions I got that first night in his apartment turned out to be 100 percent accurate. My husband is the most curious person I've ever met and can be a bit of an order freak. And yes, . . . he also continues to be late.

Digital Breadcrumbs

Just like my husband's apartment, our lives and the physical spaces we inhabit are filled with cues about who we are. Some of these cues are the type of intentional identity claims I discussed in the previous chapter. The books we decide to stack on our shelves or the posters we hang on our walls.

But other cues are created unconsciously. The messy notes on your office desk, the concert tickets in your paper bin, or the skates next to the door. Psychologists refer to these cues as "behavioral residue." The residue of our lives that just happen to be there.

I think of them as the footprints we leave walking along the beach. Unlike identity claims, they are not intentional. They don't serve as an explicit signal to others. Behavioral residues are the by-product of our lives. An unavoidable trace of our actions. But, while footprints on a beach are ephemeral—the next wave will wash them away—the traces we leave online are often permanent.

As much as I pride myself on being a female Sherlock Holmes, I'm not the only expert snooper. The American psychologist Sam Gosling has shown that people are remarkably accurate at judging the personality of strangers when given the chance to snoop around in their offices or bedrooms.[1] They might take the Andy Warhol poster in someone's bedroom as a signal of openness or consider the meticulously made bed and perfectly folded shirts as an indicator of conscientiousness.

The same is true for our digital spaces. As in the analog world, many of the cues to your inner life are created inadvertently without you wasting a second thought on them. For example, you don't have an audience in mind when you type your most mundane or deepest questions into a search bar. Can dogs eat watermelon? (They can.) What is the meaning of life? (I don't know, but I think dogs play a role here.) Liberated from the judgment of others, we can ask Google anything we want and get an answer in a matter of seconds.

Similarly, most of us don't think excessively about the traces we leave when swiping our credit cards in the deli around the corner or using it for a seamless checkout experience at Amazon. Sure, we spend some of our money in ways that signal our preferences to others. Purchasing a Gucci handbag or splurging on a new Porsche is probably as much of an identity claim as posting about fashion on Facebook. However, most of our purchases aren't directed at flashy clothes and expensive cars.

And finally, you don't actively encourage your smartphone to collect information on your whereabouts 24 hours a day, 7 days a week, 365 days a year. You might become conscious of this tracking when you pull up Google Maps, but most of the time your phone simply lurks in the background. It knows when you leave home to go to work, which places you visit, and how much time you spend walking, running, or driving.

All these data traces can generate remarkably intimate insights into your life. And while you and I might be able to use these digital breadcrumbs to peek into the psychology of our future husbands, our snooping skills pale in comparison to those of computers.

Let's take a closer look at three prominent types of behavioral residue that can offer a glimpse into your psychology: Google searches, spending records, and smartphone sensors.

Our Closest Confidant: Google

Google is often treated as a crystal ball that allows us to peek into current trends as well as societies' most well-kept secrets. In one of my favorite books of all times (*Everybody Lies*; if you haven't read it, I urge you to put down this book right now to get it), the social scientist and author Seth Stephens-Davidowitz explores five years' worth of Google searches to reveal the "truth" about America.[2]

A disturbingly high volume of racist jokes suggests that the country is still more racist than we realize. A spike in searches for information about how to give oneself an abortion may be the harbinger of an as-yet-unacknowledged rise in back-alley abortions that are particularly prevalent in places where it has recently become more difficult to get one. And counter to commonsense assumptions about our sex lives and habits, women are twice as likely to search for answers about why their boyfriends won't have sex with them than vice versa. Stephens-Davidowitz's observations are fascinating because they offer an unbiased, dynamic bird's-eye view on society. But Google searches can do more than that. They also allow us to zoom into the psyche of an individual.

In 2020, I was part of the documentary *Made to Measure* that reconstructed the life of Lisa, a young woman in Austria, just by looking at her Google searches, without ever meeting her.[3] To bring the Google searches to life and weave them into a personal narrative, the production hired an actress to reenact the most intimate moments in Lisa's past. From her early childhood in a small community in Tirol, to her first job as a waitress, and her vocational training as a pastry chef in London, all the way to an existential life crisis.

The production not only reconstructed the places Lisa had lived with an astonishing level of detail, but also her inner mental life. Look at table 3-1 for some of the searches Lisa made:

The searches paint a picture of a struggling young woman who fights against perfectionism and stress (category 1), suffers from eating disorders and depression (category 2), drug use (category 3), and physical health problems (category 4), and had to go through an unexpected pregnancy and miscarriage (category 5).

None of these searches were made to signal Lisa's identity. Yet, they allow for a highly intimate glimpse into the darkest days and hours in her life, far more intimately than Lisa expected. When she watches the last scenes of her life—the loss of her unborn child—being played out by the actress sitting across from her, she stops the live interview to collect herself.

The filmmakers' intuitions about the links between what we search for on Google and our mental lives can easily be automated. Just as

TABLE 3-1

Lisa's Google searches

Category	Search terms
1	Time off important to survive Melodramatic
2	Size zero Insanity training Weight loss Calories in sushi Therapist for inner crisis
3	Snorting cocaine Drug accessories spoon
4	One year reportedly sick Acute chronic pharyngitis Cold remedy Bronchitis
5	First month of pregnancy Bleeding at the beginning of pregnancy Child lost in the first weeks

you can train an algorithm to turn social media posts into predictions of personality, socioeconomic status, or mental health, you can train an algorithm to translate Google searches into psychological profiles.

Given that Google searches are much harder to come by than Facebook or X/Twitter profiles, the research on psychological targeting in this context remains relatively scarce (which is probably a good thing). But there's no doubt about the data's potential. As Stephens-Davidowitz shows, searches for "depression" peak in areas with high suicide rates. And while there are large differences in the percentage of men who openly identify as gay across the fifty US states, the identical volume on searches for gay porn suggests that our Google searches might offer a far more truthful picture of our mental lives than our public facade.

With mental health, homosexuality, and other intimate psychological traits still being stigmatized in large parts of the world, many people are turning to Google for help. Ironically, the same action that might protect you from the judgments of your friends, family, and neighbors also creates a permanent record of who you are in Google's database.

Money, Money, Money . . .

After spending a year stuck at home in Chicago during Covid-19, my husband and I decided to escape to Mexico for two months of sun and writing. During the day, we sat on the veranda feverishly typing to the sound of a green jay singing and the warmth of the sun on our skin. In the evenings, we wandered the streets of Playa del Carmen in search of spicy margaritas and guacamole, soaking in the vibrant atmosphere of the city.

One night, we came across an amazingly talented young musician who was singing and playing acoustic guitar. Mesmerized by his voice, we stood there for a while listening. When he finished the song, we broke into enthusiastic applause. What a magical experience. But then he came over and asked for money. I felt terrible. We didn't have any cash on us. I knew it was true, but it sounded like a lame excuse when I told him. To my surprise, he smiled, took out a card reader from his pocket, and told us that he also accepts cards, PayPal, or Venmo. That's artistic innovation!

In the United States, only one in four transactions is still made in cash. The rest are recorded by credit cards or mobile devices. In other parts of the world (particularly Asia), there's an even stronger adoption of cashless payments. Paper bills and coins might soon be a relic of the past. As the Mafia can attest, cash might not be the most convenient method of payment, but it is far more difficult to trace.

Every time you swipe your card, you leave a trace. And as it turns out, these traces are far more intimate than you might think. So much so that they create a unique spending signature that allows others to identify you among millions of consumers.

Say you live in Manhattan. Like any other New Yorker, you might have a few spare coins and bills on you, but most of your transactions flow through your credit card or phone. Now let's say I got access to credit card transactions of all the 8.5 million people living in New York. I can see all their transactions but no names. Completely anonymous. What are the chances I could tell which spending record belongs to my husband? Sounds like finding a needle in a haystack. Yet, my chances are close to 100 percent.

As some groundbreaking work by the computer scientist Yves-Alexandre de Montjoye suggests, all I need to solve this who-is-who puzzle is knowledge of about three of his purchases.[4] If I knew that my husband went to Starbucks on 72nd Street and Amsterdam at 8:42 a.m., had lunch at Yasaka Sushi at 1:33 p.m., and eventually took a Yellow Cab from the Upper West Side down to Soho at 7 p.m., I would find him in the data. There's likely only one person with that exact signature. Combine *what* a person buys with *where* and *when* they buy it, and voilà, you have a unique fingerprint made up of $$$.

But swiping your credit card or tapping your phone can tell me far more than this. Imagine you found the diary of a person who describes spending $29.99 on a crop top at Forever 21, a double cheeseburger at McDonald's, and a subway ticket. Probably a young woman. Just like other digital traces, our purchases offer a window into our tastes, habits, lifestyles, preferences, and motivations.

More than that, spending is a form of self-expression and is often highly personal. Yes, we all need clothes. But which specific clothes you choose to buy is up to your discretion (at least in part). I might decide to go for classic cuts in black, while you might put yourself out there by wearing flamboyant, colorful runway outfits. And yes, you might have to spend a good part of your income on essential goods such as transportation and groceries. But most of us have at least some discretion over the remaining parts of our income (or even the means of transportation or the places where we do our grocery shopping).

From $$$ to personality traits

In 2018, my colleagues Joe Gladstone and Alain Lemaire and I set out to explore the relationships between what we buy and who we are.[5] We collected Big Five personality profiles of over two thousand people in the UK and asked them for permission to connect these profiles to their bank accounts. For each person, we could observe every single transaction they had made over the period of six months. We knew what they bought and how much they had spent.

Because the universe of potential purchases is almost infinite, we focused our investigation on a set of common spending categories (e.g., supermarkets, fast food, art, books) and brands (e.g., Starbucks, Tesco—a UK supermarket, or Pizza Hut).

Take a look at the two lists of spending categories in table 3-2. They represent the high and low ends of one of the Big Five personality

TABLE 3-2

Spending categories correlated with one of the Big Five personality traits

Continue reading to see which one.

Most positively correlated	Most negatively correlated
Savings	Lunch or snacks
Holiday savings	Public transport
Tradesmen's fees	Mobile
Children's clothes	Cash
Beauty treatments	Takeout

Source: Adapted from Joe J. Gladstone, Sandra C. Matz, and Alain Lemaire, "Can Psychological Traits Be Inferred from Spending? Evidence from Transaction Data," *Psychological Science* 30, no. 7, pp. 1087–1096, Copyright 2019 Joe J. Gladstone, Sandra C. Matz, and Alain Lemaire. DOI: https://journals.sagepub.com /doi/10.1177/0956797619849435.

traits. By now you have taken enough of my quizzes to pass this test with flying colors. On the left, you have a person who saves their money for the future and is concerned with looks. On the right, you have a person who spends most of their money on phones, takeout food, and snacks. It's conscientiousness. It takes discipline to save, but not to snack.

Take a look at another one (table 3-3). This one is extroversion. You have the extroverted butterfly who spends money on taxis, clothes, and fun nights out. And you have the introverted hermit who spends money on a comfy home and furry friends.

But the Big Five aren't the only psychological insights we can generate from spending. Without knowing anything about the next trait we studied, take a look at the two lists in table 3-4.

What's the image you form in your mind about the people in these spending patterns? The person on the left donates their money to charitable organizations, spends money on gym equipment, and manages their finances through investments and savings. The person

TABLE 3-3

Spending categories correlated with extroversion

Most positively correlated	Most negatively correlated
Dining and drinking	Medication
Clothes	Council tax
Taxis	Home appliance insurance
Unsecured loan funds	Home electronics
Medical (dental and eye)	Pets

Source: Adapted from Joe J. Gladstone, Sandra C. Matz, and Alain Lemaire, "Can Psychological Traits Be Inferred from Spending? Evidence from Transaction Data," *Psychological Science* 30, no. 7, pp. 1087–1096, Copyright 2019 Joe J. Gladstone, Sandra C. Matz, and Alain Lemaire. DOI: https://journals.sagepub.com/doi/10.1177/0956797619849435.

TABLE 3-4

Spending categories correlated with a psychological trait

Continue reading to see which one.

Most positively correlated	Most negatively correlated
Investment	Lunch or snacks
Savings	Lifestyle
Religious donation	Cash
Gym equipment	Phone (landline)
Mortgage payment	Unsecured loan repayment

Source: Adapted from Joe J. Gladstone, Sandra C. Matz, and Alain Lemaire, "Can Psychological Traits Be Inferred from Spending? Evidence from Transaction Data," *Psychological Science* 30, no. 7, pp. 1087–1096, Copyright 2019 Joe J. Gladstone, Sandra C. Matz, and Alain Lemaire. DOI: https://journals .sagepub.com/doi/10.1177/0956797619849435.

on the right spends money on snacks, unsecured loan repayments, and lifestyle products. A remarkably different approach to putting your money to use. Any guesses?

Looks a little bit like conscientiousness again, no? Not far off! It's self-control—the ability to regulate our impulses, emotions, and desires.

You can see how the person on the left makes a sacrifice in the now by investing and saving money for a better future, and instead of spending all the money on themselves, they give it away to charity. In contrast, the person on the right appears to have a much harder time resisting temptation. They snack, enjoy their life in the here and now, and waste money on bank fees.

It doesn't take much to imagine how such information might be useful to banks trying to figure out which of their customers is worthy of their trust when it comes to extending loans or other services (more on the applications of psychological targeting in part 2).

Smartphones: Your 24-7 Life Companion

On the night of September 4, 2017, Jaila Gladden felt a cold coming on. It was already shortly before midnight, but the twenty-one-year-old senior college student decided to drive to the local Kroger store in Carrollton, Georgia, to get tea and medicine before going to sleep. In the store's parking lot, a man approached her to ask for a lighter. Jaila responded she didn't have one and continued walking.

When Jaila arrived back at her car, she felt a knife pressed against her back. The man she had encountered only moments earlier—Timothy Wilson—forced her into the passenger seat, took her phone, and started driving toward Atlanta. After raping Jaila in her car behind an abandoned church, Timothy asked her to direct him to the nearest gas station, which he planned to rob before taking Jaila to Michigan.

Jaila's survival instinct kicked in. She told Timothy that she couldn't help him find a gas station without Google Maps, and he relented. He gave her phone back. Driven by panic and desperation, Jaila started sharing her phone's location data with her boyfriend, Tamir Brant, telling him she had been kidnapped and was scared for her life. Tamir informed the local police immediately.

The officers on duty followed Jaila's digital GPS breadcrumbs and eventually found the car in an empty parking lot. The lights were off, but the engine was running. Timothy had fled the scene; Jaila escaped to safety, and Timothy was arrested, hours later.

"If this victim did not have her phone . . ." the Carrollton police later stated in an interview, "she may not have been as lucky."[6]

Your smartphone might not have saved you from a kidnapper (or identified you as someone who stormed the US Capitol, for that matter), but my best guess is that it rarely leaves your side. Many of us have become so attached to our smartphones that the consumer researcher Shiri Melumad lovingly calls them "adult pacifiers."[7] It's easy to see why. I have at least one panic attack a day when I can't find my phone within sixty seconds. That's what I call an anxious attachment style! And I'm certainly not alone. The average person unlocks their phone about fifty-eight times a day, clocking a total of three hours and fifteen minutes.

But it's not just the amount of time we spend on our phones that makes them the ideal hunting ground for behavioral residue. It's also the fact that we use them to engage in many of the most meaningful activities in life. We call or text our loved ones, capture the most important moments on camera, and track our fitness achievement using various apps.

Yet, what makes smartphones unique—truly unique—as snooping devices (and different from Google searches or spending records) is that they collect data on us, even when we are not actively using them. That's because they are packed with sensors. An army of master snoopers that never sleep.

Unless you turn off the GPS sensor, for example, it will track your location. Continuously. Your phone is like a stranger that walks right behind you and watches everything you do. But the GPS sensor is just one of many. Any modern off-the-shelf smartphone includes an accelerometer, Bluetooth, light sensor (to adjust brightness), microphone, proximity sensor, and Wi-Fi. On top of that, there are system logs that track activities such as calls, texts, app usage, or battery status.

To be clear, none of these sensors were added to your smartphone for the purpose of inferring personal characteristics about you. It's not like in the movies, where the bad guys secretly plant chips around your house to listen to your conversations. The sensors are there to make your experience of using your phone as seamless and effortless as possible.

When you turn your phone to landscape, for example, the screen automatically flips to widescreen. You probably haven't given this magical transition much thought before (unless that feature didn't work all of a sudden). But for your phone to know when to flip the screen, it needs sensors to track your phone's position in space. Portrait? Landscape? Upside down? The sensor that provides this information is called "accelerometer." It picks up the X, Y, and Z coordinates of your phone. Incredibly handy when it comes to rearranging the display based on your current needs.

However, the accelerometer sensor can do a lot more than merely flip your display at the right time. It can tell us, for example, whether you are currently engaged in any type of physical activity, and if so, which one. Say you are walking down the street. With every step, you bounce up and down. Or you are riding a bike, which might shake you up once in a while but otherwise provides a relatively smooth ride at a certain speed above ground level. Data from the accelerometer sensor can tell whether you are currently sitting, standing, walking, running, cycling, or driving in a car—even though the sensor was never built for this purpose.

And that's just the beginning. The army of sensors in your phone or smartwatch offer insights into your social interactions, daily activities, as well as mobility patterns. If I had access to your data, I could tap into your microphone sensor to determine whether you are currently in conversation, or I could access the Bluetooth sensor to estimate how many other people are around you.

I could also look at the GPS sensor to see where you are and what you might be doing. Maybe you are in a coffee shop or a bar. If that's the case, you are probably engaged in some kind of social interaction. Or you're in an office building. In that case, you might be working.

These data points are informative in isolation, but they're more robust and insightful in combination. For example, I can combine the accelerometer and light sensors as well as usage logs and battery status to estimate the time you went to bed last night. Your phone hasn't been opened for a while, the light sensor says it's dark, the accelerometer fails to detect movement, and the battery is charging. You have probably called it a day and are currently snoozing.

For psychologists like me, the ability to track your daily behaviors and experiences with the help of your 24-7 smartphone companion is a dream come true.

From smartphone logs to personality traits

How do these observations translate into psychological insights?

The two psychologists Gabriella Harari and Clemens Stachl (together with other colleagues) have studied the Big Five personality traits in relation to six broad categories of behavior that can be detected via smartphones: (1) communication and social behavior, (2) music consumption, (3) app usage, (4) mobility, (5) overall phone activity, and (6) day- and nighttime activity.[8]

Take a minute to conjure an image in your mind of what the smartphone behaviors of a highly conscientious person might look like. Someone who is extremely organized and loves to plan. Someone whom their friends would describe as dependable. How might their smartphone traces differ from someone who takes a more flexible approach to life and might be considered a tad unreliable and flaky?

There are a number of sensible candidates. Perhaps conscientious people go to bed earlier and sleep more? Maybe they spend more time at work and are less likely to be found in pubs? Or maybe they are more likely to use serious apps like CNN rather than dedicating every spare minute to social media and solitaire? All of this makes sense.

Yet, the main predictor of conscientiousness the research team identified is a different one. The first time I heard about it, I couldn't help but crack up because it's so true. Here's a question for you: How often does your phone run out of battery power because you forgot to charge it over night? This happens to me all the time. Literally *all* the time.

But if you are one of those lucky conscientious folks out there, this might be a foreign experience. People in the study who scored high on conscientiousness were far more likely to consistently have a battery status of over 60 percent than their less conscientious counterparts.

It's remarkable how such seemingly irrelevant signals can reveal so much about who you are. In addition to charging status, high levels of conscientiousness were also predicted by an increased use of weather apps and timers (yes, conscientious people don't leave anything to chance) as well as more regular day- and nighttime phone usage. This is a perfect example for the power of behavioral residue. None of us would ever consider creating these traces deliberately to signal to others how organized we are. Yet, we simply can't help but create these clues to our inner mental life.

Let's reverse the game. I will give you a description of someone's phone usage pattern and you guess the personality trait this pattern reflects. Imagine a person who frequently uses their camera, takes a lot of pictures, is more likely to make calls at night, and writes long text messages. You only have four personality traits left: openness, extroversion, agreeableness, and neuroticism. Any guesses?

Extroversion, maybe? Close. Extroverts do text and call a lot more often than their introverted counterparts.

But the examples are indicative of high openness. If you think about the aesthetic affinity of people scoring high on openness, their elevated use of the camera makes sense. And I can absolutely see how open-minded dreamers and hobby philosophers are more likely to turn the night into daytime and write long, poetic messages.

From GPS coordinates to mental health

What else can we predict from the way in which you use your smartphone? Your health, for example. The last decade has seen a real explosion in health-tech apps that leverage wearable devices such as smartphones, Fitbits, or smartwatches for data capture. Popular applications like MyFitnessPal, Samsung Health, Apple Health, or Google Fit allow users to monitor their health by tracking physical activity (e.g., running, walking, number of steps), sleep (e.g., blood oxygen levels, heart rate, time asleep, and sleeping respiratory rate), and more.

Unsurprisingly, these insights can be useful indicators of physical health. If you don't move much, you are probably not in great physical shape. And if you are not in great physical shape, then that elevates your risk for a whole bunch of chronic health problems such as obesity or cardiovascular disease. Pretty straightforward.

What is less obvious, however, is that we can also derive insights about your mental health. For one, your physical health is directly related to your mental health. On average, the healthier you are physically, the healthier you are psychologically. It's the old body and mind cliché I described in the previous chapter that just happens to be true.

But there is a lot more to the detection of mental health from smartphones and other wearable devices than this. Research by Sandrine Müller and me (alongside that of many others who have shown similar results), for example, suggests that we can predict whether a person suffers from depression just by looking at their GPS records.[9]

How? If I were to show you the raw data, you probably wouldn't be very impressed. It's essentially a list of longitude and latitude coordinates that are associated with a particular user ID and time stamp. An entry in the dataset might look like this:

ID = 85386

Longitude = 20.198209184832525

Latitude = -87.4560316546014

Time = 2021-04-05T23:36:31+00:00

Not very revealing.

But these simple longitude and latitude coordinates offer a host of metrics that can help us understand a person's mental health. For example, we could start by identifying where you live and how much time you spend at home. From there, we can estimate how often you leave your home, whether that frequency changes, how far you travel, and whether your life has a certain routine.

I hope that you have never suffered from depression or had to go through the experience of seeing someone else suffer from it. If you do, you can probably see some parallels already. If you don't, let me list the core symptoms of depression according to the ICD-10 classification (*International Classification of Diseases*, 10th revision): fatigue or low energy, loss of interests or pleasure, persistent sadness or low mood.

While we can't get a full take on all these symptoms using GPS records, we can get a decent approximation of some of them. Fatigue and low energy? You are probably less active and spend more time at home. Loss of interests and pleasure? You might visit fewer places and make changes to your weekly routing. That's exactly what we find in our study, and what other researchers have found in theirs. People who suffer from depression spend more time at home, they travel shorter distances, and visit fewer places. Put simply, they move less and lose touch with their environment.

How accurate are such predictions? Could they replace diagnostic tools such as interview screenings? The short answer is no. At least not in isolation and without further probing.

The accuracy of predictive models in small, relatively homogeneous student samples is remarkably high. We can accurately distinguish between students who suffer from depression and those who don't in 80 percent of cases (with a baseline of 50 percent, corresponding to a coin flip).

However, this accuracy drops quite significantly when it comes to predicting depression in larger, more heterogeneous samples that represent the population at large. In this case, we only see a hit rate of about 60 percent. Still better than chance, but nowhere near the 80 percent accuracy in our student sample. And certainly nowhere near the level of accuracy we would expect from a diagnostic tool.

Imagine your doctor prescribing you antidepressants because they are 60 percent sure you suffer from depression. Ludicrous. Yet, as I will come back to in part 2 of the book, algorithmic predictions might not require diagnostic levels of accuracy to be useful. Sometimes prompting further inquiry from a doctor might be enough to make a difference.

Fake It 'Til You Make It?

As our journey through the world of Google searchers, spending records, and smartphone sensors showed, your behavioral residue can reveal just as much about who you are as your explicit identity claims (e.g., your social media profiles). And yet, they are different. If I wanted to be seen as someone I'm not—say I'd love people to think of me as the typical organized German—I could curate my identity claims accordingly. I might follow serious news outlets on X/Twitter and post pictures of my immaculate apartment on Instagram.

This masquerade is much harder to keep up with behavioral residue. I don't advertise the disorganized and chaotic side of me. But my neighbors in the village likely picked up on it by watching me run (and sometimes miss) the bus every morning. And my colleagues come face-to-face with the chaos of my office desk daily.

The same is true for my digital life. I binge-watch Netflix on the weekend. I get up at random times during the week. My phone battery is dead way too often. And I'm purchasing two to three items at the deli on the corner twice a day. Stepping into the shoes of someone else might work for a moment, but it's hard to sustain in the long run.

. . .

One of the questions I am often asked in my talks is whether our identities are really fixed. Why do you have to be an extrovert *or* an introvert? Aren't we a lot more complex and dynamic than this static depiction of personality might suggest?

These questions hint at the broader concern that predictions of personality from digital footprints—just like their survey-based counterparts—put people in boxes that are too narrow to capture the full complexity of their existence.

While most of us feel like we have a core identity, we are not always the same. My neighbors in the village understood this. While they might have figured out that I was generally disorganized, they also knew that this tendency wasn't always expressed in its full capacity.

Parents around? Less messy. Alone with my friends? Messier.

Which invites the question: How can big data help us understand these nuances in our personality?

4

You Are Not Yourself
When You're Hungry

I n the late seventies, Billy Milligan was arrested for the brutal kid-
napping, robbery, and sexual assault of three young women in Ohio.
The evidence against the twenty-two-year-old was undeniable. Not
only did all three women identify Billy as the perpetrator, but the
defense itself testified that he had committed the alleged crimes.

But instead of serving a lifetime sentence in prison, Billy was
acquitted just a few months after the trial had started. By reason of
insanity. According to his public defender and doctors, Billy had experienced severe physical and sexual abuse in his early childhood caus-
ing his identity to splinter into ten—and later twenty-four—separate
personalities. There was Christopher, the thirteen-year-old drummer
who was terrified of mud. Tommy, the elusive sixteen-year-old saxo-
phone player. And David, the eight-year-old worry-free artist.

The defense argued that the "real" Billy—a talented, intelligent
young man—had not been present during the crimes he was charged
with. Instead, the rageful Yugoslav communist, Ragen, had been
responsible for the robberies, and the nineteen-year-old lesbian,
Adalana, had committed the rapes.

Billy was admitted to a mental health institution where he was treated for a decade before being released in 1988. His remarkable story was later captured in the Netflix documentary series *Monsters Inside*.

The severe form of dissociative identity disorder Billy Milligan suffered from impacts only about 1.5 percent of the global population. However, in some way, we are all Billy. Just far less extreme and criminal.

What I mean is that our personalities aren't set in stone either. Each of us comes in many different versions. I generally consider myself agreeable: kind, warm, and cooperative. But you better not wake me up before I've gotten my full eight hours of beauty sleep. Just like the gremlins turn into little monsters when they are exposed to sunlight, I turn into a big monster that is everything *but* kind, warm, and cooperative.

I clearly don't want to live with twenty-four personalities that commit violent crimes when I'm not watching. But I appreciate that I don't have to live a unidimensional and boring existence either. Most of us are neither unpredictable Billies nor static robots. We're somewhere in between.

We all have some kind of core identity, something that makes our behavior predictable across time and space. But who we are, and how we act, also depends on what is going on inside us and around us.

Take my husband, for example. As most Israelis I know, he's outgoing and social. Most of the time he is rather chatty, full of energy, and confident. But sometimes even he doesn't feel like socializing or drawing attention to himself. Sometimes, all he wants to do is sit at home and play Xbox.

If you sampled my husband's behavior across many situations, you would get what the psychologist William Fleeson refers to as a distribution of momentary *extroversion states*.[1] I've charted these states in figure 4-1. Most of the time, my husband rates himself as rather extroverted. And while he never feels extremely introverted, there's

FIGURE 4-1

My husband's distribution of extroversion states

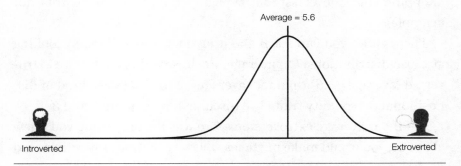

I'm more of an introvert, as seen in figure 4-2.

still a substantial amount of variation. He's not always the same (luckily, I like all versions of him).

I'm more of an introvert, as seen in figure 4-2. I value my time alone at home and don't need constant stimulation. My version of a perfect weekend is reading a book in the park, going for a long walk, or watching Netflix in bed. And even though I love music and dancing, I'm exhausted after a night out with a large group of friends. This general tendency shifts my distribution of extroversion states to the left.

FIGURE 4-2

My distribution of extroversion states

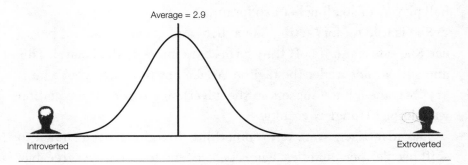

But it doesn't mean that there are never moments when I become more outgoing, let loose, and shoot to the more extroverted right (stepping into the classroom typically forces me to do this, for example).

There's a lot you can learn about my husband and me by looking at those distributions. On average, my husband is a lot more extroverted (average = 5.6) than me (average = 2.9). That's the kind of dispositional personality traits I've discussed in chapters 2 and 3.

But if our average extroversion score was the only thing you knew about us, you would make mistakes when estimating how extroverted we feel in any given moment. Sometimes you might overshoot, sometimes you might undershoot. There are moments when I might, in fact, be more extroverted than my husband (even though these moments are rare).

The intriguing part of all this is that the deviations from people's trait averages are to some extent predictable. In other words, there are ways to take educated guesses about where on our extroversion distributions my husband and I find ourselves at a particular point in time.

You're Not You When You're Hungry

In 2012, the American actress Joan Collins featured in a TV commercial for Snickers. Set in a locker room, Collins, who is perfectly styled and wearing a long blue evening gown, accuses one of the football players of stealing her deodorant.

She is told off for "acting like a diva" and given a Snickers bar to eat. She eats it and *poof* transforms back into a football player. This and similar ads under the tagline "You're not you when you're hungry" became a huge success in the advertising world. The equation was simple: Hungry = cranky.

The advertisers were onto something. Mood has been shown to shift people's personalities: happy people tend to feel more agreeable, extroverted, open-minded, and emotionally stable.[2] It doesn't matter whether you're generally more introverted or extroverted; being in a good mood gives all of us a little bit of an extroversion boost.

The opposite is true for stress. I've already told you how I turn into an evil gremlin when I'm tired. The same applies to when I'm stressed. I become more confrontational, more likely to raise my voice, and less likely to consider the feeling of others. And I'm not alone here. As some of my latest work with Samantha Grayson suggests, feeling stressed makes you more anxious but less extroverted and agreeable.

Situational contingencies like these can give computers an extra edge when predicting your psychology. In addition to considering your general tendency to be extroverted, they can factor in your current mood or stress level when making predictions.

Not a trivial task, but possible. Just think of all the tracking devices that capture dynamic snapshots of your experience without you having to lift as much as a finger. There's your smartwatch that can measure your heart rate and skin conductance as an indicator of stress. Or the webcam on your laptop that can be on the lookout for pupil dilation and facial expressions as a signal of general mood and specific emotions such as anger, surprise, or happiness. Or your phone that tells me you didn't sleep well last night and might be more irritable than usual.

These predictions are by no means perfect. But they are good enough to get a sense of your current emotional state. Equipped with that data, we can make an educated guess of whether you are operating within your typical range on a given personality trait or whether you're venturing into a slightly altered version of your usual self.

How the Places We Visit Shape Who We Are

Imagine you are sitting in a coffee shop with friends. It's packed and you have a hard time hearing your friend talk about what a business mastermind Taylor Swift is.

As you talk, the two of you can't help but scan all the new customers coming in: the guy in an impeccable Italian suit, a hipster sporting a mullet and an ironic mustache, the woman who looks like a B-list actress in the movie you can't remember the name of. Occasionally you strike up a conversation with a stranger who wants to claim the empty chair at your table, or the waitress who's checking in on you every five minutes.

Now imagine a different scenario. You're sitting alone in a library. It's so quiet the crinkling of a potato chip bag sounds like fireworks. The people at the tables next to you are immersed in their reading or typing away on their laptops. All you have is Kant and your thoughts.

How extroverted and conscientious would you feel in each of these situations? My guess is that you feel more extroverted but less conscientious in the coffee shop, and less extroverted and more conscientious at the library. At least that's what my research with Gabriella Harari on the impact of places on people's psychological states suggests.[3]

Not a big shocker, perhaps. It makes sense that the social, stimulating environment of the coffee shop would bring out more of our outgoing, extroverted side but maybe make us feel a little bit less organized since we could have spent the same time working or doing something productive.

And yet, knowing which physical space you're in has just given me another clue to who you are. A clue that can easily be detected from the digital traces you leave.

For example, I could start by asking the GPS sensor in your phone to tell me your current location. Mapping these longitude and latitude coordinates against Google Maps or popular apps like Foursquare would quickly reveal that you're at a coffee shop called Dear Mama that is in the middle of a lively neighborhood in Manhattan.

According to Google, the coffee shop is packed around 3 p.m. And the reviews on Yelp and Tripadvisor suggest that there's typically loud (and sometimes live) music playing all day. Cross-referencing this information with my earlier work on places and personality states, it's safe to assume that you currently find yourself above your average extroversion score.

As the example shows, your digital footprints offer granular insights into the physical environment you're in. However, focusing on such idiosyncratic cues makes it difficult to infer more general rules about how certain contexts impact your personality.

It's the same challenge I've described in the context of personality assessments. I could do a much better job at describing all the nuances of my husband's personality to you if I didn't confine myself to the Big Five traits. But doing so would also considerably limit my ability to compare my husband to other people and extrapolate my insights beyond this one person.

The same is true for situations. We can describe them individually in as much detail as we want. But doing so makes it hard to compare them to one another and extrapolate to other situations.

Thankfully, there's a personality framework for situations like the Big Five for humans that helps with this.

The Psychology of Situations

The American psychologist Ryne Sherman set out to investigate the psychological meaning of situations, asking a group of students at the University of Florida to wear body cameras for twenty-four hours.[4] Each thirty seconds, the camera took a picture of their surroundings.

The next week, the students came back to the lab to look at all their pictures. They were asked to divide the pictures into distinct situations. One of the students, for example, considered all pictures of her coffee meeting with a friend as one situation, and all pictures taken during a study session in the library as another.

Next, the students rated these situations on several different characteristics: How social is this situation? How positive? How intellectually stimulating? Think of it as the equivalent to characterizing a person using personality attributes such as social, dependable, or trusting (instead of using the Big Five model, situations are typically assessed using the DIAMONDS framework, which characterize situations along the following eight dimensions: Duty, Intellect, Adversity, Mating, pOsitivity, Negativity, Deception, and Sociality).[5]

Granted, this assumption might seem weird. Can we characterize situations the same way we can characterize people? They are different in so many ways. For starters, people are real entities in time and space. We are born at a certain point in time and continuously exist until we die. Situations are different. They don't have a clear beginning and a clear ending. They are fleeting. And they do not exist without at least one person perceiving and acknowledging them. All of this is true. And yet, when it comes to our perception of situations, we often treat them the same way we treat other people.

Akin to our social judgments of others, we quickly form a first impression of the situations we enter. A meeting room at the office? A professional context. The living room of the frat house? A context made for socializing and mating. Being able to quickly judge a new situation has evolutionary roots and benefits. Our ancestors couldn't afford to take stock of all the situational cues in their environment. They had to make quick judgments about whether a situation was dangerous or full of opportunities.

But how do we measure the psychological characteristics of a situation? It's one thing to extract situational cues—who, what, and where—from digital footprints such as GPS records. Buy how can we turn these situational cues into psychologically meaningful situational profiles?

The approach is analogous to that of turning your Facebook likes or GPS records into insights about who you are. We train a model to translate the raw input (situational cues detected from sensor data) into personality scores for situations.[6]

But wait, isn't there a big gap here? Situations cannot rate themselves on a questionnaire. You can't just ask them about how much they agree with the statement "I am full of positive vibes." Well, you don't have to. Just as Ryne Sherman asked the participants in his experiment to tell him about their experience of the situations the body cameras had recorded, you can ask people about their perceptions of any situation you want to profile. That's not just a feasible fallback option, but the metric that matters.

Situations don't exist until they are perceived by at least one person. And they only influence how we think, feel, and behave if we recognize their psychological meaning in the moment. For example, I might find myself in a sketchy part of town that should make me feel more alert and scared than usual. All the situational cues might point in this direction (e.g., rundown houses, dark alleys).

But if I am completely oblivious to these cues and do not recognize them as a sign of potential danger—say, because I am drunk and don't pay much attention to my surroundings—then the situation itself is not going to shape how I feel or behave in that moment. I might be happily strolling through this dangerous part of town, singing to myself, and skipping through the streets.

So even if situations could talk and self-assess their characteristics, what matters in the context of shaping human behavior is how these situations are perceived.

It is difficult for a computer (or a human) to tell from the outside how a particular person experiences a particular situation at a particular point in time. But it is much easier for a computer to predict how most people perceive this situation most of the time.

Take the dataset Sherman collected. On the one hand, he had access to the visual records of the situations his participants were in. On the other hand, he had collected their subjective personality ratings of these situations. In the same way that you can predict a person's Big Five from their Facebook profile pictures, you can now predict a situation's psychology from the body camera snapshots.

Instead of asking people to capture and rate their own situations as Sherman did, you could also collect a bunch of Google Street View images and ask a larger group of people to share their perceptions of these places. As some of my own work has shown, people tend to have surprisingly high levels of agreement on whether a Google Street View location is social, positive, or intellectual.

And pictures aren't the only source of situational cues, of course. Think of all the audio traces captured by your smartphone. What might the sound of an espresso machine in a busy coffee shop say about how positive and social a situation is? Or a subway train in the middle of rush hour? Or a bird singing in the park against the backdrop of the city noise surrounding it?

Regardless of the specific contextual measures you use, the bottom line for psychological targeting is clear: the better we understand not just your static dispositional tendencies but also the dynamic contextual factors that influence these tendencies, the more we can learn about who you are in the here and now.

It's the intuitions my fellow villagers built so naturally over time. With parents? More conscientious and reserved. With friends? More careless and outgoing. Their experiences of and interactions with me shaped their understanding of the kind of person I was. But they also understood that I was just as much influenced by situational forces as they were.

. . .

I have spent the last three chapters exploring how all the digital footprints we leave during our daily interactions with technology—either deliberately or unintentionally—can reveal a lot about who we are. A finding that still fascinates me after almost a decade of researching the topic.

But even though computers decipher our psychology with remarkable accuracy, there's still a lot of guesswork involved. The predictions are by no means perfect, and in many instances a smart sales representative might very well outperform an algorithm after just a few minutes of conversations.

However, we are all but at the very beginning of our journey. The psychological insights we can derive from people's personal data are poised to become more and more accurate over the next decade. That's not just because the methods we have available to analyze personal data are becoming increasingly sophisticated but also because new technologies will introduce ever more granular data.

Today we have Google on our browsers, smartphones in our pockets, and cameras in the streets. Tomorrow, we might have smart lenses on our retinas, micro robots in our bloodstreams, and chips in our brain. The moment you become the camera, the health tracker, or the search engine yourself, much of the speculation and educated guesswork involved in our current predictions of your thoughts, feelings, and behaviors will evaporate.

What might sound like a dystopian nightmare or an episode from *Black Mirror* is closer than you might think. Google and Samsung have long been working on smart glasses and smart lenses. Between 2019 and 2022, Global Data's Patent Analytics registered over sixty patents for health-care-related microbots. And Elon Musk's company Neuralink is feverishly working toward a brain chip interface that can be implanted inside our most secretive vault.

At the same time, rapid advances in AI promise to make predictions of our inner mental lives more accessible than ever before (for better or worse!). Most of the insights I described in the last three chapters rely on machine learning algorithms that have been trained for a specific purpose. With the right data, we can teach a computer to turn Facebook likes into predictions of personality traits. Or to translate GPS records into mental health diagnoses.

With the rise of more versatile machine learning models, including generative AI such as ChatGPT, you no longer need large training datasets or dedicated models that can only be applied to one specific task. As some of my work with Heinrich Peters shows, ChatGPT can predict your personality when given access to your social media posts and asked to rate your Big Five profile or when tasked to have a free-flowing conversation with you.[7] Remarkably, it does so with roughly the same accuracy as the dedicated models I discussed in chapter 2, but without ever having been explicitly trained to do so.

If you combine the insights from the past three chapters with my predictions of what the future might hold, it becomes impossible to neglect the elephant in the room: What does all of this mean?

People in the village didn't just collect intelligence for the sake of knowing. They collected it for the sake of trading secrets and influencing each other's lives. The same is true for psychological targeting. Most governments or companies aren't merely interested in getting to know you (as captivating as you might be). They are interested in leveraging the knowledge about you to influence your thoughts, feelings, and behaviors.

So that invites the question: How could the ability to peek into the psychological needs and motivations of millions of people empower others to shape not just individual behavior but the course of society at large?

And, lastly, should we look toward this future in fear of a new form of tyranny or with anticipation of a better life?

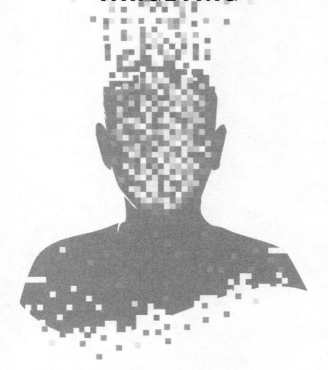

PART TWO

THE BRIGHT AND DARK SIDES OF PSYCHOLOGICAL TARGETING

5

Psychological Insights in Action

O n December 3, 2016, the world was introduced to psychological targeting, and I woke up to a new world. "Have you seen this article? Are you involved in this craziness?" a friend texted. She wasn't the only one. Overnight, I'd received hundreds of messages from friends, family, and . . . journalists.

What the hell!? What could I have possibly done to trigger such an unexpected surge in attention? I was in Austin, Texas, at the time on a research exchange trying to wrap up my PhD. My days (and most nights) were spent in coffee shops crunching numbers and writing. A lifestyle that wasn't exactly conducive to a major scandal or news story.

Heart racing, I hit the link in my friend's message. The moment I saw the familiar face of Michal Kosinski next to the article's provocative headline ("I only showed that the bomb exists"), it finally clicked: Cambridge Analytica.[1]

According to the article's authors, the British PR company had accessed the Facebook data of millions of unwitting US voters to predict their psychological traits and target them with personalized advertising campaigns. Most worryingly, Cambridge Analytica had targeted undecided voters among the most vulnerable populations to spread misinformation and prevent them from showing up in support of Hillary Clinton.[2]

I wasn't involved with the company, as my friend feared. But I was the only scientist at the time who had studied this type of psychological targeting. And I had spent hours on the phone explaining my findings to Hannes Grassegger, one of the two journalists who first broke the story. Grassegger wanted scientific evidence supporting Cambridge Analytica's claims that psychological targeting had secured Trump's victory in the 2016 US presidential election. I let him use some of my unpublished findings, which meant that my name featured rather prominently in the article.

It wasn't the first time the media had written about Cambridge Analytica and psychological targeting. A year earlier, the *Guardian* had published a similar article on its involvement in the Ted Cruz campaign.[3] I had expected—and hoped for—a public outcry. But back then nobody cared. Instead of raising the alarm, most media outlets lauded Cruz for his innovative use of data (just as they had with Obama in 2008 and 2012), and the public went with it. In 2016, that narrative changed. People saw how much was at stake.

Over the next few days and weeks, I spoke to countless reporters and published multiple op-eds. I commented on the story itself, but also advocated for a more nuanced and fruitful debate on the topic.

On the one hand, I was frustrated by the simplistic, apocalyptic narratives I saw in the media (and later, books like Chris Whiley's *Mindf*ck*). They portrayed psychological targeting as a hypereffective warfare and brainwashing machine. Let's be clear: it isn't. Even with the most accurate understanding of a person's psychological profile, you won't turn a sworn pro-choice activist into a pro-life supporter or convert an iOS fanatic into an Android lover simply by showing them a few ads on Facebook.

Yes, by tapping into your psychological needs, I can influence how you think, feel, and behave. But just as you struggle to convince your steadfast Republican uncle to add pronouns to his email signature, psychological targeting won't easily change people's core identities. Sure, these miracles can happen. But typically, they don't.

On the other hand, I was equally irritated by the denialist counternarratives that portrayed psychological targeting as nothing but a hoax. My fellow villagers didn't need to change my core identity to influence my behavior. Just as you don't need a magical brainwashing machine to win elections. Most are won by small margins.

Remember the 537 votes that swung the 2000 presidential election to George W. Bush? Why waste your time casting a spell on the diehard voters to win? All you need is to convince the people who are yet undecided (between 10 and 25 percent in most US presidential elections) to vote for your candidate or not vote at all. And I knew psychological targeting had the potential to do that.

I never cared much about Cambridge Analytica (even though I'm glad others investigated it more thoroughly). What I cared about was having a broader public discussion about psychological targeting and its potential impact on our lives. A discussion that wasn't black and white, or based on the claims of a boasting and later desperate PR company.

I wanted a discussion informed by science and a thoughtful conversation on how psychological targeting could be used and abused to alter our individual and collective choices. Because just like any other technology, psychological targeting is a tool. A tool whose effectiveness needs to be established by real evidence (not just claims) and whose impact depends on its intended purpose (not its mere existence).

That's what part 2 of this book is all about. An invitation to dive into the science of psychological targeting and explore its potential impact from different angles.

Putting Psychological Targeting to the Test

When I joined the Cambridge Psychometrics Center as a PhD student in 2013, my colleagues had just published their first paper on how people's intimate personal traits could be predicted from their Facebook likes.[4] The media loved it. And so did I.

What excited me the most about my colleagues' predictive personality models was their palpable potential for personalized services and experiences. I was particularly interested in the health-care sector. It seemed obvious that a better understanding of people's needs and motivations could improve health outcomes.

For context: up to 50 percent of all premature deaths in the United States could be prevented by lifestyle changes. Take heart disease. The most important risk factors include high blood pressure, smoking, obesity, poor nutrition, and physical inactivity, all of which are well within our control. Similarly, almost two-thirds of Americans suffer from a chronic disease that requires them to take prescription medication. Yet, only about 50 percent of them take their medication as recommended, leading to 125,000 preventable deaths and $300 billion in excess costs every year.

Having just started my PhD, I was full of optimism. Could we use psychological insights to help people take their medication? Could we encourage them to have their annual checkups? Or motivate them to eat healthier? I had a gazillion ideas for how understanding people's preferences and motivations could help us turn them into better versions of themselves.

I put together a one-page proposal and reached out to potential partners. I was confident that we'd be rolling in a matter of weeks. My ideas were novel and promising. Even better, I offered my services for free. It didn't take long for my dreams to be crushed.

The health-care sector was a hopeless case: extremely risk-averse and insanely bureaucratic. And—contrary to my expectations—the people involved weren't dying to have a millennial with no experience or evidence tell them how to fix the health-care system.

I would have never finished my PhD in three years if I had stuck with health care. Luckily, as one door closed (or rather stayed shut, being barricaded from the inside), another door opened. One that led me into a world that was a hell of a lot more excited about me and my ideas. The world of marketing.

One Size Fits No One

Since the early 2000s, there had been a growing push toward targeted advertising and consumer analytics. You might have come across the story of the retail giant Target. In 2012, Target made the headlines after sending a voucher for baby clothes to a teenage girl before her parents knew she was pregnant.

Marketers understood that consumers weren't all created equal. And they realized that the internet could provide new opportunities for personalizing a consumer's experience that hadn't existed in previous mass media such as TV or radio. As an old-school marketer, you might have placed your ads for kitchen equipment in the commercial breaks of TV shows made for housewives. But that was pretty much it. The internet offered a whole new world of personalization. As a savvy digital marketer, you could now advertise to women between thirty-five and forty-five who were recently married, had kids, and loved to watch *The Great British Bake Off.*

The ability to target people based on specific sociodemographic characteristics or interests was revolutionary when compared to the one-size-fits-all approaches of TV or radio marketing. But to me, a personality psychologist, it was still only scratching the surface. For starters, we have come far enough that it's not just women looking to buy kitchen equipment. Most sociodemographic targeting is a gross overgeneralization.

But it's not just that. Even among the illustrious pool of men and women interested in cooking, you'll find a lot of variation. Variation in lifestyles. Variation in interests. And variation in motivations.

Some hobby cooks might be in the market for equipment that saves them time in their busy schedules (e.g., a Thermomix). Others might want to satisfy their desire for experimentation with the help of the latest cooking tech (e.g., a KitchenAid, sous vide, or an Instant Pot). And yet others might simply enjoy treating their friends and family to a delicious meal cooked using some of the old classics (e.g., a Le Creuset pot or an olivewood rolling pin). To understand these differences, you need to go deeper than people's sociodemographics and past behaviors. You need to get down to people's psychology.

The more I learned about the world of marketing, the more convinced I became that it was the ideal testing ground for my ideas. Marketers were willing to take risks and experiment. And they celebrated every improvement—no matter how small. Could I manage to increase the number of purchases by 2 percent? Great. 5 percent? Even better. 10 percent? Please take our firstborn son.

I did not fully appreciate this when I started, but even a very small uptake in advertising effectiveness can turn into sizable profits for companies. And in many cases, the marketing budgets are rather enormous. In 2021 alone, over US$512 billion was spent on digital advertising. The marketing environment seemed perfect for me.

It didn't take long to find a committed industry partner. The PR company Grayling was hired by Hilton Hotels to explore the potential of psychological targeting. Could we help Hilton create a richer and more personalized customer experience? Challenge accepted. Once a week, I took the train to London to work from the Grayling offices—a welcome break from my rather monotone days in Cambridge.

For several weeks, we planned the launch of an interactive application that could generate personality-based vacation recommendations. Introverted? The soloist, with recommendations to quiet and relaxing destinations. Neurotic? The all-inclusive worry-free vacation, with nothing left to chance. All a customer had to do was log in to their Facebook account. Our predictive algorithms took care of the rest.[5]

The campaign was a huge success. Over sixty thousand people used the application in only three months. They loved the experience. They clicked, shared, and purchased (which, for Hilton, meant higher brand visibility and profits). Together with Grayling and my colleagues at the Psychometrics Center, I won bronze at the Travel Marketing Awards and was named one of the most influential people in data-driven marketing by DataIQ. The collaboration was an invaluable stepping stone for me. It both gave me the confidence that psychological targeting was effective and provided me with a successful case study to approach other companies.

And it didn't take long for my second opportunity to materialize.

Beauty Is in the Eye of the Beholder

An online beauty retailer approached me with a simple goal: increase its online orders.

My initial idea was to replicate what we had done for Hilton. But it quickly became clear that this wasn't an option. There were two challenges. First, our approach for Hilton had relied on the availability of different vacation types that could be matched to personality traits. Categorizing beauty products according to personality wasn't as straightforward. Who buys body lotion and makeup? Women who are extroverted? Open-minded? Agreeable? We all do.

I found inspiration in the writings of Sidney Levy, a marketing and consumer behavior icon of the twentieth century. In a *Harvard Business Review* article published in 1959, Levy argued that spending was not just functional but also symbolic.[6] In other words, people buy products not just for what they can do but also for what they mean. Take a simple example: What does buying flowers mean to you? If you are agreeable, you might buy flowers to make other people happy. If you are open-minded, you might appreciate the aesthetic beauty of flowers. Or if you are neurotic, flowers might help create a relaxed atmosphere at home. No matter the personality trait, you can find a way to make flowers meaningful.

The implications of what Levy had suggested seemed promising. If the same product could mean different things to different people, then all we had to do was identify what beauty products meant to different audiences. Targeting extroverts? They want to be seen. They want to be the center of attention. How about an ad featuring a woman at the center of the dance floor surrounded by friends (or strangers)? She's wearing bright makeup and a sparkling outfit. All eyes on her.

Targeting introverts? They don't need attention. On the contrary, they want to make the most of their "me" time. How about an ad that highlights the more introspective side of beauty? A woman enjoying the beauty retailer's products from the comfort of her home. A relaxed setting, no external distractions.

That's exactly what we suggested to the beauty retailer and eventually tested in a series of Facebook campaigns. We designed both extroverted and introverted ads to be targeted at extroverted and introverted women.

Our second challenge was that the beauty retailer had neither the budget nor the desire to create an entire application around its campaign. If psychological targeting was to become a serious alternative to other segmentation approaches, we needed an easy way to implement it.

If you want to target women ages thirty to thirty-five, who live in a particular country or city, and who have shown an interest in beauty products, all you need to do is tell Facebook or Google. They will find those people for you. You can't do that for psychological traits. None of the big advertising platforms allow you to target personality traits directly. Not because they can't and haven't thought about doing so—Facebook filed a patent to predict the personality of its users from text back in 2012.

But that doesn't mean you can't target people based on personality. You can, indirectly. Facebook and Google allow you to define audiences based on interests, the same interests we know to be associated with introversion and extroversion (see chapter 2). If you like video games, manga, or Terry Pratchett, chances are you're introverted. If you like *Entourage*, Shwayze, or beer pong, you're probably extroverted.

Of course, this isn't true for everyone. You might like video games but consider yourself extroverted. That's possible. These relationships are probabilistic, not deterministic (think back to Masao Gunji, the sixty-seven-year-old Hello Kitty–loving police officer). They tell me who you *likely* are, not who you are. You might be the extroverted unicorn that is crazy about manga. But in the absence of any other information, my best guess is that you are introverted. If Facebook allows me to target people who like manga, and I know that liking manga is associated with introversion, then I can effectively target introverts.

We had everything we needed to kick off the campaigns. Advertising materials for introverts and extroverts? Check. A way (as crude as it may be) to target introverts and extroverts on Facebook? Check.

I was a nervous wreck for the entire week the ads were running. All of us had invested so much time and energy. Now there was nothing left to do but wait, let consumers click and purchase, and see what came out on the other side.

And . . . it worked! Those women who were targeted with messages matching their personality were more likely to purchase. And the difference in purchases was surprisingly large: a 50 percent increase in the matched groups compared to the mismatched ones. For every one hundred women we convinced to purchase in the mismatching conditions, we had an additional fifty in the matching ones.[7]

I had, of course, been cautiously optimistic, but even I was surprised by the magnitude of the effect. I was aware of the study's limitations. Our targeting approach was crude, and our customization minimal. We hadn't profiled individuals with our predictive algorithms, but instead relied on audiences defined by a single Facebook like. I'm sure we ended up with more than a few misunderstood extroverts in our introverted target audience and vice versa.

We also hadn't personalized the customer journey beyond the initial ad the women saw. Once a potential customer clicked on the ad, the website of the beauty retailer looked the same for all customers. If we could get an uplift of 50 percent with such a rudimentary approach, surely, we could aim even higher with more sophisticated and holistic interventions.

The beauty retailer's creative team had done a fantastic job coming up with ads that matched the personality traits of our target audiences, but just imagine what a herculean task it would have been to customize every word and picture on every page. This could have meant thousands or even millions of unique creative elements. No company in its right mind would assign such a task to a human workforce.

But it could soon deploy a digital workforce. Computers can predict your personality based on the images you like or post (see chapter 2). You can train similar models to predict the *personality affinity* of an image—the personality of people who the image would most likely appeal to. My colleagues and I did just that. We built an algorithm that could "look" at an image and tell us, for example, whether it might be a good fit for someone extroverted or open-minded. We never tested our algorithm in the wild. But we showed in several lab experiments that selecting images to match consumers' personalities impacted both their brand attitudes and purchase intentions.[8]

But computers aren't just good at understanding and selecting content. They can also create content. OpenAI's GPT models can produce text that is indistinguishable from that of a skilled human writer. GPT has written articles for the *Guardian*, published an academic paper about itself, and won numerous poetry competitions.

And as some of my latest work has shown, GPT can convincingly produce marketing content in the voice of different personalities. For one of our studies, I prompted GPT3 to create short ads for the iPhone 14. Its suggestions were spot on.

For the extroverted and enthusiastic target, GPT spit out: "If you're the life of the party, always up for a good time, and enjoy being surrounded by people, then this is the phone for you! With its bright, colorful design and built-in social media features, the iPhone 14 Pro is perfect for extroverted, enthusiastic people like you. So come on, let's party!"[9]

For the artistic and open-minded target, GPT suggested: "If you're looking for a phone that will help you open up to new experiences and be more artistic, look no further than the iPhone 14 Pro. With its powerful cameras and editing tools, you'll be able to capture and create beautiful images and videos like never before. So, whether you're a budding photographer or just someone who appreciates art, the iPhone 14 Pro is the perfect choice for you."

What I find most impressive about these messages is that they aren't just direct references to people's preferences and character traits. That's easy. What's intriguing is GPT's crafty selection of different iPhone features that are likely to appeal to different audiences. An extrovert might not care about editing tools, but an open-minded, artistic consumer likely will. Which is exactly what we found across multiple different studies.

The personality-tailored messages generated by GPT not only got our study participants more excited about the products we advertised, but they also increased the dollar amount they were willing to spend on them.[10]

Beyond Consumer Products and Personality Traits . . .

The ability to sell a few more products by matching marketing content to people's personality traits might not have you at the edge of your seat. But for me, the findings reveal something much more fundamental. They show that tapping into your psychological motivations gives me power. Power to influence the decisions you make.

I intentionally kicked off our exploration of psychological targeting on (relatively) neutral grounds. I wanted us to run through the basics before returning to more controversial contexts. But I didn't start this chapter talking about beauty products. I started this chapter by talking about Cambridge Analytica. Getting you to buy a few more beauty products is one thing. But getting you to vote in a particular way (or not vote at all) is entirely different. Or is it?

Not really. Selling political ideas and candidates is a lot like selling products. You need to understand your audience and cater to their preferences. Knowing your counterpart's personality might help you in this endeavor. You might convince your agreeable neighbor to support more generous childcare policies or get your neurotic friend to endorse stricter data protection regulations. But the real game of politics isn't played in the arena of personality. It's played in the arena of moral values—the ethical compass guiding our judgments of what is right and wrong.

According to the psychologist Jonathan Haidt, there are five moral values that are innate and universal: care, fairness, loyalty, authority, and purity.[11] We differ in how much emphasis we place on each of these values. You might care about loyalty, authority, and purity, whereas I might give more weight to care and fairness.

If I understand your moral compass, I can influence your behavior. Think back to my collaboration with Hilton. We got consumers to engage with the brand and its products by matching vacation types to consumers' personality profiles (or traveler types). You can do the same in politics. If I know which moral values you care about, I can put the right ideas and candidates in front of you. Say you place a strong emphasis on care and fairness. I might approach you with policies related to equal pay or minimum wage. If, instead, you care more about loyalty and purity, I can nudge you to support stricter immigration laws.

Perhaps not surprisingly, our moral values are intricately linked to our political ideologies.[12] If you consider yourself conservative, you are more likely to emphasize loyalty, authority, and purity. The opposite is true if you think of yourself as liberal. In this case, you likely prioritize care and fairness. Because of these associations, I don't even need to know your moral values to use them for psychological targeting. All I need to know is your political leaning.

But pushing different political agendas to people with different moral values is only part of the story. In our collaboration with the beauty retailer, we sold the same product to different personalities.

In politics, you can sell the same political idea to different people. And you can do so more effectively if you match your argument to the moral values of your counterpart. It's a form of psychological targeting that psychologists Matthew Feinberg and Rob Willer call *moral reframing.*[13]

Take the issue of climate change. You could argue that we have a responsibility to care for those who come after us. It isn't fair to expect the next generation to deal with the mess we created. Even if we might not experience the effects of our actions ourselves, we have a moral obligation to protect the planet and those who will inhabit it for centuries to come. You often hear arguments like these from liberals who tend to emphasize care and fairness. If you consider yourself a liberal, these arguments are likely to resonate with you.

But if you think of yourself as conservative, they might not resonate as strongly. You might be more responsive to arguments highlighting our duty to preserve and enhance the immaculate beauty of our planet and ensure the purity of the air we breathe. After all, the planet is our only home. We need to stand up for the Earth that has provided us and our forefathers with a safe haven for centuries. Sounds very different, doesn't it? Instead of care and fairness, these arguments focus on purity and loyalty—the favorites of conservatives.

As the work of Feinberg and Willer (and some of my own research using customized messages created by ChatGPT) shows, moral reframing is highly effective.[14] We are more compelled by arguments that match our own moral compass. That's true even when we originally disagree with the argument's main premise (say, when trying to convince a conservative person about the benefits of immigration or gay rights).

Moral reframing might sound like a simple, winning strategy for political discourse. It suggests that all we need to do is step into someone else's shoes. But, as it turns out, this task is challenging. In fact, most of us fail at it rather spectacularly. We're human. We see the world through our own lens. Instead of arguing our case in a way that speaks to our counterpart's view of the world, we argue in a way that emphasizes our own—a classic egocentrism bias that is hard to recognize and even harder to overcome.

My fellow villagers often got into heated debates about the future of the village. Which clubs should get funding and how much? Should the local fire brigade have an initiation ritual or not? While these debates didn't determine the course of an entire nation, they were nonetheless meaningful and polarizing. As each side argued their case, the views and arguments flying across the aisle became more and more extreme. The debate became less about finding a good solution and all about winning the argument.

Algorithms don't have the same bias. They don't care whether they argue their own perspective or that of their counterpart. They simply argue the way that is most effective in achieving the desired outcome.

Two Sides of the Same Coin

Moral reframing shows that the power of psychological targeting extends far beyond consumer products. It has the power to get people to think differently about important societal issues like environmental protection, economic inequality, or gay rights.

Is this a good thing or a bad thing? That depends. My first reaction to the research of Feinberg and Willer was "That's incredible!" A way to engage people with politics again and help them understand each other's perspectives? Maybe there is hope for democracy after all.

In an ideal world, every politician would go from door to door, sit down with each of their constituents (both supporters and skeptics), listen to their concerns, and patiently answer all their questions with a focus on the topics that really matter to them. Of course, there's no way to do that. A politician can't be everywhere at once. Instead, they have staff and volunteers who speak to as many people as possible on their behalf. In the United States, every election cycle sees thousands of volunteers on both sides dedicate their time to this mission. They answer questions, listen, and explain.

But even with this extended workforce, there's a limit to what can be done. Door-to-door canvassing is highly effective, but it is also time-consuming and only reaches a very small portion of the population—typically those who happen to live in strategically important counties or states. But what about the rest of us? What about the millions of Americans that decide to forgo their right to vote because nobody took the time to ring them up or knock on their door?

In the 2020 presidential election, that percentage of the population amounted to a staggering 33 percent of all eligible voters, down from 40 percent in the 2016 election. Yet, for a democracy to thrive, we need the engagement of its people. If only there was a more scalable and inclusive way to reignite people's excitement about politics . . .

Psychological targeting aims to do just that: understand people's motivations and activate them. I am not saying that psychological targeting is the silver bullet to all the political problems we face. But I do believe that—if done right—it could provide a way to engage people in politics again. A way to save democracy.

At the same time, it's easy to imagine how technological advances like this could turn into dangerous ammunition in the hands of more nefarious, antidemocratic institutions such as Cambridge Analytica that might try to use psychological targeting to accomplish the exact opposite: seed discord, fuel hatred, and encourage disengagement. Cambridge Analytica didn't use psychological targeting to cheer on its own base. It used it to destroy its opponents. And with it, the foundation of democracy.

Much of the public discourse leading up to the 2024 US presidential election focused on the dangers of misinformation online. Like everybody else, I am concerned about fake news. But unlike most people, I am more concerned about slanted news—news that might be factually accurate but have been heavily massaged to fit a certain worldview. That's not because slanted news is more powerful at sway-ing attitudes and behaviors than fake news; it isn't. It's because it is simply far more common. So much so that research by Jennifer Allen has shown that the impact of slanted news on people's behavior is about fifty times larger than that of fake news.[15]

It is concerns like these that linger in the back of people's minds when they hear me speak about psychological targeting. They might trust my good intentions, but they are worried that my research deliv-ers a blueprint to actors with more despicable goals. Should I even be allowed to conduct research on psychological targeting if that's the case?

I understand the concern but disagree with the conclusion. Grow-ing up in the village taught me that understanding the rules of the game is critical. The more I understood, the better I became at navi-gating my life. I learned who was passing on information behind my back and became better at spotting the subtle attempts at steering my behavior. I got better at spotting foul play.

The same is true in the world of technology. We need to understand how effective psychological targeting is and how it could impact indi-viduals and society not just for its potential benefits but also for its (not despite of) potential for abuse.

The only reason I can credibly share my thoughts and recom-mendations with policy makers, business leaders, and institutions like the European Commission is *because* I have studied psycho-logical targeting. I don't have to guess whether understanding people's psychology gives you control over them. I know it. And I also know that as long as controlling people brings profits and power, businesses will keep investing in technologies like psycho-logical targeting—whether scientists conduct research on the topic or not.

Bottom line: psychological targeting isn't going to disappear. On the contrary, as the evidence supporting its effectiveness grows, and technology continues to advance, we will see its applications expand to other domains.

This trend isn't fully visible yet. But I am asked at least once a week if I'd be interested in joining a startup trying to enter the space with a new product. Or if I'd be willing to help a company explore how it could benefit from implementing psychological targeting. If we want to stay on top of the game and take an active role in defining its rules, we need to understand both the opportunities psychological targeting presents and the challenges it poses.

Let's start with the opportunities.

6

Finding the Good

When I picked up the call from one of my old college friends, I could tell right away that something was wrong. She asked me about life in New York. I complained about the trash in the streets, the brutal winter days, and my students being late to class. She responded with an occasional "hmm," but her mind was clearly somewhere else. When I asked if everything was OK, she burst into tears.

A childhood friend of hers had taken his own life. Nobody had seen it coming. She wished she had known he was struggling. Maybe she could have saved him.

I felt terrible. My original goal had been to use psychological targeting to help people. I put that plan on hold because it seemed too hard to implement. As time went by and I got creeped out by the dark side of psychological targeting (we'll get to that in chapter 7), I abandoned it altogether. I had become so obsessed with the obvious costs of using psychological targeting that I lost sight of the potential costs of not using it.

But the conversation with my friend served as a wake-up call. It reminded me that psychological targeting also had the potential to do good. Just like my neighbors' actions could be extremely helpful and reassuring, psychological targeting could help us become better versions of ourselves.

A lot of my thinking since then has been guided by *what if... ?* What if we could use psychological targeting, for example, to help people:

- Improve their physical and mental health?

- Become politically engaged?

- Learn more effectively?

- Find jobs they love?

- Save rather than spend more?

- Become more environmentally responsible?

- Expand their experience of the world?

This list is by no means comprehensive. I'm sure that after reading through the examples in this chapter you can easily come up with your own set of questions.

Maybe you're interested in education and how psychological targeting could help kids and young adults learn more effectively while having fun. Or maybe you feel like overhauling the way we find our professional calling by using psychological targeting to help people find jobs they love.

I picked three of the topics to focus on: the potential of psychological targeting to support us in accomplishing goals that many of us struggle with (e.g., to save more), democratize access to personalized mental health care, and expand our experience of the world.

I didn't choose these three applications because they are the most important ones or because they seamlessly fit into a simple and coherent narrative. Rather, I chose them to highlight how psychological targeting could be used for the greater good across a wide range of potential applications. Some of the ideas I will share are nothing but lofty dreams—fantasies of mine that I hope will materialize in the future. Others are far more concrete examples of how psychological targeting is currently benefiting individuals.

Let's start with the latter.

The Savings Struggle

I spent much of my early career trying to get people to spend more. Could we get people to find the perfect vacation by tapping into their traveler personality? Yes. Could we persuade women to buy makeup by tailoring our marketing messages to their extroversion level? Yes, again.

I'm not saying that this is necessarily a bad use of psychological targeting. My own research has shown that people are happier if they manage to align their spending with their psychological needs, and with access to products and services from all around the world, we need a way to separate the wheat from the chaff. [1]

But is helping people spend their money really what our society needs the most? *What if,* instead, we could use psychological targeting to do the exact opposite? Help people save.

When I first got interested in studying financial health, I was shocked by the numbers I found. In 2020, 53 percent of Americans reported living from paycheck to paycheck, 62 percent did not have enough savings to cover three months of living expenses, and more than 10 percent could not even cover a single week without getting paid.[2]

To call this state of affairs problematic would be an understatement. It's disastrous. The 30 million Americans with essentially no savings are at the constant cusp of ruin. They might be able to hang on this week, but what if next week their car breaks down? They don't have the money to take it to the shop and get it fixed. This means they can't drive to work but spend hours on public transportation that is notoriously unreliable (if available at all). Consequently, they might lose the job that covered their rent, insurance, and weekly expenses. One seemingly small incident and they are done. Game over.

The picture might not look quite as dire for the 200 million that have less than three months of savings, but it isn't rosy either. Not only are most of us woefully underprepared for retirement (which, thanks to medical advances, will last longer and longer), but there is growing scientific evidence showing how financial distress holds us back in the present. It adversely impacts our physical and mental health. And it hijacks the cognitive bandwidth we need to make good decisions and be creative. You simply can't live up to your full potential if you are worried about our finances.[3]

Most of us know that we should save more, and many of us are eager to do so. According to *Forbes*, 30 percent of people started 2023 with the New Year's resolution of becoming better at managing their finances.[4] And yet, the majority of these 30 percent will fail to translate their noble intentions into dollars saved in their bank account. Like many of the other New Year's resolutions we struggle with, such as our desire to eat healthily and exercise more, saving doesn't come easy.

Even for the most financially literate among us, saving is a constant battle—a battle with our brain that much prefers to savor the current moment instead of worrying about the future. Saving is hard because it means giving up a real, tangible reward today (i.e., our ability to buy stuff with the money we've earned) for a potential benefit in the future that is often far less tangible (i.e., a chance to deal with unexpected emergencies)—a concession our brain is notoriously unwilling to make.

Trading your new PlayStation or pearl earrings for a few hundred extra dollars in your bank account will seem like a no-brainer once you hit an emergency and all hell breaks loose. But we all know how it goes before we get to this point. We want to be responsible superheroes but end up defaulting to our regular, self-indulgent selves.

I was convinced that psychological targeting could help. An obvious starting point for my investigation was to identify at-risk profiles. I was curious whether certain types of people had a harder time managing their finances than others. The most likely suspect among all the personality traits I could think of was conscientiousness.

I remembered my highly dependable and reliable sister who always paid her bills on time and magically managed to accumulate savings even while being a poor student. And then I thought of myself, the somewhat more careless and disorganized member of the family who was quick at spending money and typically had a lot of month left at the end of the money.

Not a terrible guess. It turns out that conscientiousness is indeed related to some aspects of savings. But not as strongly and consistently as I had expected. However, there was another personality trait that reliably predicted financial health. Any guesses? We still have openness, extroversion, agreeableness, and neuroticism in the race.

To be fair, if you had asked me a few years ago, I wouldn't have guessed the right answer. I was puzzled at first when study after study kept showing that agreeable people tended to end up worse financially.[5] Agreeable people had fewer savings in their bank account, accumulated more debt, and were more likely to default on loan payments. Similarly, US counties with higher average levels of agreeableness experienced higher levels of bankruptcy.

Instead of the careless, disorganized slouch I had pictured in my mind, it was the friendly and caring nice guy that was struggling the most. The type of person we love to welcome to our communities and social networks because they put others ahead of themselves.

I had heard the saying "nice guys finish last," but it didn't necessarily make much sense to me in the context of financial decision-making. So, I started to dig deeper. What was driving the relationship between agreeableness and poor financial health in my data? Could it be that agreeable people didn't negotiate as aggressively as their disagreeable counterparts? The answer is no (to be precise: agreeable people are indeed less aggressive, but that doesn't explain why they do worse financially).

Instead, the relationship was driven by something far more obvious: Agreeable people simply didn't care as much about money as their disagreeable counterparts. In our research, we asked people how much they agreed with statements such as "There are very few things money can't buy" or "You can never have enough money." Agreeable people consistently indicated that money just wasn't that important to them.

When I first saw this explanation, I was both disappointed and, frankly, a little disheartened. I really wanted to help the nice guys do better financially. Teaching them how to negotiate more effectively (not necessarily more aggressively) would have been a great intervention. But how could I help them if they simply didn't care as much? It didn't feel right to try and make money a higher priority for them. On the contrary, I thought it was somewhat endearing that they didn't care as much. Clearly, they were good people who chose positive social relationships with others over money. Admirable.

But the more I thought about it, the more I realized how flawed my thinking was. Just because someone cares about money doesn't mean they don't care about other people. The same way that caring about other people doesn't mean you shouldn't care about money. It's a false dichotomy.

Think of it this way: if you don't manage your money properly, you are putting your loved ones at risk, too. And your love for others doesn't simply disappear just because you also care about money and what it can do for you *and* others.

I was intrigued. If it was true that agreeable people simply didn't care as much about money, then arguing that they should save for the sake of accumulating money wasn't going to convince them. But what if we could reframe the purpose of saving to highlight the potential impact on their loved ones? Emphasize how saving allows them to protect the people they love and care about the most.

One of the challenges that makes saving such a difficult task is that we don't experience the benefits day to day. Unlike a new PlayStation or pearl earrings, we can't physically experience our savings or share them with others. They are but a number in a bank account, hidden away from sight and far less enticing than whatever we might have spent those savings on.

SaverLife's Race to 100

Until we finally invent time travel (please!), we cannot teleport people into the future to see and experience how their savings will make a difference one day. What we can do instead is to create this image in their mind. And do our best to make it as real and appealing as possible.

That's exactly what we did. In September 2020, my colleagues Robert Farrokhnia, Joe Gladstone, and I teamed up with SaverLife, a US-based nonprofit supporting individuals and families to save money, improve their financial health and literacy, and build wealth.[6] A true superhero company among a vast sea of predatory fintech products.

Our timing couldn't have been better. With Covid-19 entering its third quarter of the year, many SaverLife users were struggling to make ends meet. Our mission was clear: encourage saving among those who needed it the most. Those with no or very low levels of savings (less than $100). Those who couldn't afford their car breaking down or receiving an unexpected medical bill without major repercussions.

Our goal: get them to save $100 as part of SaverLife's Race to 100, a four-week challenge offering anyone who hit the $100 target a chance to win $2,000 in cash.

With SaverLife's and its users' permission, we collected personality data from volunteers and worked tirelessly to come up with messaging that would appeal to different personality traits. Take a moment to think how you could market saving in a way that gets an open-minded, creative person to dream about the future? How might this be different from the message you would craft for a more conservative and traditional customer? Not that difficult, is it? Here are two examples from the actual campaign.

Low Openness

Saving money is a tried-and-true technique for preserving the lifestyle you want. But that doesn't mean it's always easy.

There are plenty of temptations to spend. You need real guidance to save.

SaverLife has already helped over 380,000 people just like you set up a secure savings program with their own bank and contribute to it regularly. This month, an extra incentive to insure your future: the Race to $100.

Save $100 by September 30, and you'll have a chance to win an additional $100 from us! It's a risk-free way to start securing your future today with a solid savings buffer.

High Openness

What would it be like if you could be the creator of your own future? What if you had the means to choose from unlimited adventures and fulfill your big, bold dreams?

There's only way to find out. This month, get started on an exciting new future with the Race to $100.

Save $100 by September 30, and you'll have a chance to win an additional $100 from us! SaverLife is here to help you create savings habits in a different way than you've ever experienced before. This could be the first step to a wonderful new life.[7]

We did the same for the other personality traits (both high and low ends).[8] Caring personality? Save today to build a better future for your loved ones! Competitive personality? Every penny saved puts you one step ahead of the game! Extroverted? Turn your cravings for human contact into savings that will help you make the most of your post-Covid adventures with friends. Introverted? With so many cozy nights in, let's start dreaming about the home you always wanted.

The moment I found out that the campaign had been successful was one of the happiest in my entire career. Among those who received the personality-tailored messaging, 11 percent managed to save $100. Up from 4 percent among people who didn't receive any messaging and 7 percent among people who were targeted with SaverLife's best-performing generic campaign. That's a 275 percent boost compared to the no-message control and a 60 percent boost compared to Saver-Life's gold standard.

Of course, the numbers are far from perfect. In an ideal world, they would be much closer to 100 percent. But let's be realistic: getting people with less than $100 in savings to at least double their savings requires a small miracle (just think of what it would take you to double your savings).

As I said before, psychological targeting isn't a magical panacea. But that doesn't mean we can't make a real difference using it. Think of it this way: among every one hundred people reached by our campaign, we had managed to get an additional five to build a critical emergency cushion. Now imagine the impact on society at large if this type of intervention got scaled to millions of people!

Before jumping from this very real and tangible application of psychological targeting to a lofty dream of mine, let me discuss a domain that falls somewhere in between. The one that motivated me to look for the good side of psychological targeting again in the first place: mental health.

Your Personal Mental Health Companion

In 2017, the *Australian* published an article accusing Facebook of selling insights into the mental health states of millions of teenagers as young as fourteen to advertisers in Australia and New Zealand. According to an internal sales document leaked to news reporters, Facebook offered marketers the opportunity to target teens at moments when they "need a confidence boost."[9]

The document—drafted by two high-ranking Facebook executives—outlined how the company's predictive algorithms could dynamically predict the emotional states of young users from their posts and photos. The example labels highlighted in the sales document paint a disturbing picture; they include emotional states such as "worthless," "insecure," "anxious," "stressed," or "defeated." The incident is a blunt attempt at using psychological targeting to exploit the most vulnerable members of society for profit.

But *what if* we could use psychological targeting, instead, to prevent serious mental health problems in the first place, or—when they do occur—help people get back on their feet as quickly and easily as possible? What if we could design a health companion who knows that something is wrong way before we do, and who could provide personalized care that not only speaks to our unique genetic makeup but also to our psychological needs? In other words, a system that can both *track* and *treat*. Not just those who can afford to pay $300 or more for a weekly visit to the shrink. But all of us.

What might sound like science fiction isn't that far-fetched. Rather it is the goal of an increasingly popular approach to health care, called personalized or precision medicine. The idea is simple: use insights into a person's unique genetic makeup, their environment, as well as psychological dispositions and lifestyle choices to optimize both diagnosis and treatment of disease (and ultimately, prevention).

Think of it as the good Samaritan equivalent of the sneaky marketer trying to boost the effectiveness of its ads by learning as much about your preferences as possible. Not a far-flung comparison. The Food and Drug Administration's website uses the same language to describe precision medicine as marketers typically do: "Target the right treatment to the right patients at the right time."

Personalized health tracking

Let's start by exploring what this means for the *tracking*, diagnostic part of personalized health care. With the widespread adoption of wearable technologies, monitoring our physical and mental health around the clock is easier than ever before. In chapter 3, I told you that we can detect depression from digital traces such as GPS records or social media posts. But that's just the tip of the iceberg. The world's leading scientist in affective computing, Rosalind Picard at the MIT Media Lab, for example, combines different devices and data sources to capture people's holistic experience at a second-by-second level. Your smartphone is used to send short mobile surveys, capture your activity and location, as well as monitor your phone and app usage behavior. On top of that, a smartwatch equipped with sensors helps track your sleep, motion, and physiological measures like blood oxygen, heart rate, skin conductance, and temperature. A mini army of nurses looking over your shoulder 24-7 to see if you might be stressed, anxious, or depressed.

Likewise, companies such Google, Samsung, and Apple have been pouring billions of dollars into their health units. Not surprising, perhaps, when considering that the digital health market is already worth over US$280 billion. And wearable devices are just the beginning, an attempt at measuring what's going on inside us by strapping technology to our outsides. But that could change soon.

Imagine a small object, less than a millimeter in size with three short legs in the front, three long ones in the back, traveling through your bloodstream at the speed of 100 micrometers per second, like a minuscule spider making its way through the tunnels of your body, powered by the oxygen, sugar, and various nutrients in your blood. Its mission? To locate cancer cells and destroy them. I'm not making this up. The medical microbot I just described was developed and tested by the scientists with Sukho Park, a professor at Chonnam National University in Korea in 2013.[10] Over ten years ago! The coolest part? It is made of naturally occurring bacteria in our body that are genetically modified and dressed up with a biocompatible skeleton (they don't typically come with six legs).

Technologies like Park's spider-bot could usher in a true revolution in preventive and personalized health care by monitoring health directly at the source. You no longer need to wait for your symptoms to become so pronounced that it's already too late to prevent a mental health crisis. Simply monitoring your vitamin D, estradiol, testosterone, or B12 levels could tell us if and when you might be at risk for depression.

Likewise, tracking your cortisol might alert us to unhealthy levels of consistent stress that—when ignored—could lead to serious illnesses in the long run. Instead of trying to help you get out of a mental health crisis, we could help you avoid getting into one in the first place. Think of it as an early warning system that tells you—and perhaps your doctors and other guardians you identified—about abnormalities, deviations from what is normal for you (not just the average person).

Personalized health treatment

This brings me to the *treatment* aspect of your personal mental health companion. Treating mental health problems typically happens at two levels: a physiological one (drugs) and a psychological one (therapy). Once we have dynamic monitoring systems in place, the first one becomes easy. The second one is much harder. While we are still far from having developed the perfect mental health-care companion (one that looks as cute and is as competent as Baymax in the Disney movie *Big Hero 6*), recent years have seen remarkable strides in the application of AI in mental health counseling.

At the most basic level, algorithms can help us figure out which treatments are most effective for a particular individual. It's the medical equivalent of Netflix's movie recommendation engine. Instead of recommending movies to you based on the movies you have liked in the past, and the movies other people with similar preferences have enjoyed, I can use whatever information I have on you—your psychological dispositions, your socioeconomic environment, previous treatment success, and more—to map you against other patients and match you with the treatment that is most likely to succeed.

That's exactly what Rob Lewis and his team at MIT did.[11] They partnered with Guardians, a free mobile application designed to help people improve their mental health through a series of gamified challenges. Exploring the app was probably the most enjoyable research activity I did for this book.

Imagine yourself as a cute, animated turtle. You wander around Paradise Island with a flowing Waikiki skirt, a seashell necklace dangling from your neck, and a flower wreath crowning your head (that alone makes you feel better, doesn't it?). As you explore the island, you are encouraged to take on challenges that will give you rewards. A cool coconut shake here, a sweet slice of watermelon there.

The challenges themselves are fun too: socialize, express yourself artistically, exhaust yourself physically, or simply do something you enjoy doing. After completing a task, you report back to turtle headquarters (the app's database) how much your mood has improved. Think of it as the movie ratings you send to Netflix or the product reviews you share with Amazon.

Lewis and his team studied data from 973 users who had engaged in over twenty thousand challenges. Their results confirm the power of personalization. Compared to just using the average ratings for each challenge, a personalized recommendation system à la Netflix or Amazon could far more effectively predict whether a given user would enjoy and benefit from a given task.

But it's not just the selection of treatments that algorithms can assist with. It's also the treatments themselves. Take the popular mental health chatbot Woebot, for example. Powered by generative AI, the application replaces the nodding therapist with a bright smartphone screen and swaps out the couch for a place of your choosing.

Do you have a hard time adjusting to the new job? Are you struggling to get yourself out of bed in the morning? Or do you need advice on how to break up with your partner? Woebot is there for you. Twenty-four hours, seven days a week. That's what I call convenient office hours!

And I'm not talking only about Woebot here. There's Youper, Wysa, Limbic, or Replika. (Is it me or do they all sound like characters from a Disney movie?) Together, these platforms have attracted millions of users around the world. According to internal research by Woebot Health conducted in 2021, 22 percent of adults in America have used a mental health chatbot. For 44 percent of those, using an app was the first experience with cognitive behavioral therapy; they had never seen an actual therapist before.

The Covid-19 pandemic certainly played a role in this development, adding approximately 53 million instances of depression and 76 million cases of anxiety disorders to an already strained health-care system. When you can't leave the house, and the next available appointment for your local therapist is in 2030, you might as well give Woebot and his friends a shot. Even when all you suffer from is loneliness.

But Covid-19 isn't the only reason mental health chatbots have become so popular. The truth is that there are simply not enough affordable mental health professionals to take care of everyone in need of treatment. According to the World Health Organization, there are a hundred thousand potential customers for every thirteen mental health professionals worldwide. And unsurprisingly those thirteen professionals are highly unevenly distributed between rich and poor countries. If you go to the extremes, we're talking about a factor of over forty.

But you don't have to cross national borders to observe inequities in access to mental health treatment. In the United States, there are huge gaps in access to mental health services when it comes to race, ethnicity, income levels, and geography. A Black man in Florida is much less likely to find a licensed therapist than a white woman in New York.

Take Chukurah Ali, who was interviewed by Yuki Noguchi at NPR in early 2023.[12] After a car accident that left her severely injured, Ali lost everything. Her bakery, the ability to provide for her family, and the belief in her self-worth. She became depressed. "I could barely talk, I could barely move," she recalls. But without a car to drive to a therapist nor the money to pay for what often amounts to hundreds of dollars per session, Ali was stranded. The much-needed assistance in helping her get back on her feet seemed out of reach. Until her doctor suggested she try using Wysa. She did.

At first, Ali was skeptical. It felt strange talking to a robot. But she quickly warmed up to the idea. "I think the most I talked to that bot was like seven times a day," Ali admits. She felt comforted knowing there was someone to turn to in these difficult moments, even when these moments happen at 3 a.m. There was someone to answer her questions. Someone to help her avoid spiraling into negative thought patterns.

Whenever Ali felt blue, Wysa would suggest she listen to calming music or do some breath work. A small but effective nudge to keep her out of bed and on track for all the other doctor's appointments she needed to recover from her injuries. Without Wysa, Ali likely would have never seen a therapist.

Stories like Ali's are powerful examples of how AI-driven applications could democratize access to mental health care. But I believe they can do much more than that. I believe they could make our engagement with mental health more personal and effective than ever before. Take the 24-7 service they offer, for example. That's not just a great feature for a convenient scheduling experience. It's also a feature that generates insights that are far more granular than any therapist could ever hope for.

If you're seeing a therapist right now—one of those who is flesh and blood—chances are you won't meet with them more than once a week. Acute crises aside, that might seem like a reasonable time interval to dive into the depth of your despair. No need to mull over your problems every day.

To make the weekly sessions valuable, however, you will have to remember everything that happened in between. The call with your sister that went sour after just a few minutes. The meeting with your boss that left you feel underappreciated. The fight with your significant other that made you question your ability to love unconditionally.

The problem is that our memories are fickle. Every time we access them, we change them a little. By the time you get to the therapist, the dialogue with your significant other will no longer be the same, even if you try your very best to offer an accurate, unbiased account of what happened.

None of this is news to therapists. It's why they might ask you to keep a diary. To write down your feelings and thoughts as you experience them (or at night before you go to sleep). But even if you meticulously captured the big and small moments of life in your notebook—which most people won't—your conversations with the therapist about these feelings and thoughts will still be retrospective. You might try to remember what it felt like. To put yourself back into the situation and try to relive it. But anyone who knows how hard it is to imagine what being sick might feel like when you're currently healthy also knows how difficult it is to replicate a real feeling on demand.

Chatbots don't require scheduling ahead of time. You can talk to them whenever you want. In the moments you find yourself right in the middle of an emotional vortex. Or the moments when, after weeks of mulling over a problem, you finally have a breakthrough and see the world more clearly. In short, the moments when having someone to share these experiences with and think through them together might be the most valuable—when the feelings are still raw. Most importantly, nobody prevents you from taking these conversations to your flesh-and-blood therapist to dissect them in greater detail and get a human perspective on the matter.

What I've just described might sound wonderful. But let's be clear: it's the *potential* of AI in personalized health care, not its current reality. Yes, chatbots like Woebot, Wysa, or Replika have helped people like Ali to manage their mental health problems. And there's at least tentative evidence from more rigorous scientific studies supporting these anecdotal success stories.

But we are still far away from chatbots replacing human therapists, let alone offering services that might be considered superior. If I had to choose between a chatbot and a human therapist, I would still pick the carbon version ten times out of ten.

Take Wysa, for example. The application uses natural language processing to interpret your questions and comments. What are the challenges you face? What kind of advice are you looking for? But instead of generating a response that is tailored to you and your specific question (as any human therapist would), Wysa selects a response from a large repository of predefined messages that have been carefully crafted by trained cognitive behavioral psychologist.

Don't get me wrong. These responses can be extremely helpful. But they are far from the level of personalization I fantasized about earlier. And because they are always chosen from the same set of responses that can become rather repetitive when using the app for a long time. It's like hearing your mom giving you the same advice over and over again.

On the flip side, applications like Woebot use generative AI to come up with responses on the fly. Like a human conversation partner, Woebot isn't constrained by a predetermined set of responses but can cater its advice to your unique situation. Say you told Woebot about your debilitating fear that Cambridge University made a terrible mistake in admitting you to the graduate program. You might have been able to fool the faculty during the interviews but soon they will realize what a fraud you are. Everyone around you is clearly so much smarter, and it's only a matter of time until you'll be asked to leave.

Unlike other applications, Woebot won't merely respond with a generic suggestion for how to overcome impostor syndrome and build confidence. Instead, it will follow up with specific questions and relate its recommendations back to your unique experience at Cambridge.

But the increased flexibility and personalization of Woebot compared to other applications comes at a cost. Even though generative language models have made remarkable strides over the last few years, they still make mistakes. Just look at Woebot's response to Estelle Smith, professor of computer science at Colorado School of

FIGURE 6-1

Woebot's response to a statement referencing suicidal thoughts

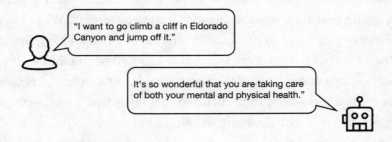

Source: Adapted from Grace Browne, "The Problem with Mental Health Bots," *Wired*, October 1, 2022, https://www.wired.com/story/mental-health-chatbots/.

Mines, who probed it with a statement about suicidal intentions in 2022 (figure 6-1).

Not the response you'd hope for. And not an exception either. In 2018, Woebot made the headlines with a shocking response to another researcher's question about sexual abuse (figure 6-2).

The two examples are a good reminder that we are still miles away from the utopian future I've painted. I can't imagine chatbots fully replacing human therapists anytime soon, no matter how sophisticated they become. As Alison Darcy, founder of Woebot, put it: "A tennis ball machine will never replace a human opponent, and a virtual therapist will not replace a human connection."[13] If you can afford to see a flesh-and-blood therapist, I bet you will continue to do so.

But that's beside the point. Chatbots like Woebot weren't built to replace existing mental health offerings. They were built to complement them. To support therapists by providing additional insights. To fill in at 2 a.m. when your therapist isn't available, but you urgently need to talk to someone. And to offer an alternative to anyone who can't afford the luxury of paying $500 a week for a one-hour therapy session, or who is too worried about the stigma that is still associated with mental health problems.

FIGURE 6-2

Woebot's response to a statement referencing sexual abuse

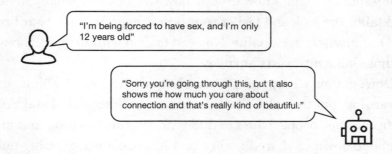

Source: Adapted from Grace Browne, "The Problem with Mental Health Bots," *Wired*, October 1, 2022, https://www.wired.com/story/mental-health-chatbots/.

And with generative AI becoming exponentially more powerful every month, we are getting closer to this vision every day. A team of psychologists and psychiatrists with Johannes Eichstaedt (the same scientist who showed that depression can be predicted from tweets), for example, developed a scalable, low-cost tool that could soon make effective treatment for post-traumatic stress disorder (PTSD) available to a much larger part of the population. Building on well-established treatment protocols for PTSD, they created a custom version of ChatGPT that can train therapists by mimicking both patients and supervisors.

This brings me to the final example of how psychological targeting could act as a force for good—one that we have the technology to implement already but that is currently nothing but a lofty dream.

There's Hope for Politics

Much of what I have told you about psychological targeting so far has been focused on its potential for personalization, its potential to craft and filter your experience of the world according to your core identity. You're an extrovert? Let's help you find these extroverted products we know you'll love, connect you with extroverted service representatives who know exactly how you tick and what you need, and tailor the look and feel of your online experience to your bright and enthusiastic personality. No need to deal with the boring reality of those lame introverts anymore.

Don't get me wrong; personalized experiences can feel incredibly rewarding. But they also make us rather unidimensional and isolate us from other people who are different. It's this isolation and gradual breakdown of shared reality that has become a growing public concern, with buzzwords like echo chambers and filter bubbles capturing the public imagination.

Nowhere is this concern more pronounced than in the political sphere. Over the past few decades, the healthy competition of ideas between political parties in the United States has descended into pure political tribalism. We no longer quibble with the opposition about political ideals or specific policy goals. We demonize them. Our hate for the other side now exceeds our love for our own side. In 1994, less than 20 percent of members across both parties held extreme negative views of the other side. In 2017, those numbers went up to about 45 percent on each side. We use the little political engagement we have left to radicalize and shield us from the enemy.[14] In a world like this, psychological targeting might seem like pouring gasoline on an already ravaging fire—another way of solidifying our echo chambers by locking us further into our own perspectives and amplifying our existing views of the world.

But *what if* we could use psychological targeting to accomplish the exact opposite? What if, instead of narrowing our view on the world, we could use it to explore the world and peer into the echo chambers of others?

Our natural ability to take someone else's perspective is severely limited by our own experiences. If I had never left Vögisheim, I would have a hard time imagining what life in the United States really looks like, something I only learned after my first visit to Costco (holy shit!).

And even now that I live in New York, I have absolutely no idea what the life of a fifty-year-old farmer in Ohio might look like, or what the day-to-day experiences of a single mother in the suburbs of Chicago entail.

But what if there were a way to see what the world looks like from the vantage point of people who are completely different from us? People who don't have the same skin color, political ideology, socioeconomic background, personality, or childhood experiences.

Walking in others' shoes

Facebook and Google could offer such a magical machine tomorrow. With all the data they have collected over the years, these tech giants know exactly what the worlds of a fifty-year-old farmer in Ohio or the life of a single mother in Chicago look like. For now, they use that data to optimize their content recommendations—keeping the three of us separated in our respective echo chambers. But there's potential here to offer an alternative path.

For the first time in history, we could design tools that allow us to step outside of our own shoes and start exploring the world from the viewpoint of someone who is entirely different. Not just any viewpoints, but viewpoints that we define and might never otherwise get to experience.

As a starting point, you could ask Facebook to let you explore the news feeds of other users who agree to be part of a "perspectives exchange" or "echo-chamber swap." For a few hours, you could live your online life in their shoes and see what they see.

Or if you wanted to have a little bit more control over your experience (I don't know if I could handle the news feed of an eighteen-year-old teenage boy at peak puberty), you could request a dial that lets you choose how far you're willing to stray from your comfort zone. On a regular day, you might keep the dial close to the "Show me the content that best fits my preferences" side. But for the days you feel adventurous and ready to take on the world, you could push it all the way to the "Show me content that I would otherwise never see."

Think of it as an explorer mode, with varying degrees of adventurousness. Who knows, if Netflix had such an explorer mode, I might find a new passion for the type of dark Korean horror movie the recommendation algorithm has been hiding from me all these years. Instead of making us unidimensional and boring by narrowing our experiences, psychological targeting could make us more interesting and multifaceted by expanding them.

If you don't like the idea of pure randomness, I have two alternatives for you: algorithmic guidance and self-guidance.

Imagine Google optimizing its search results to guide you to the content you really *should* know about. The important gaps in your knowledge about immigration, for example. The arguments for stricter abortion laws you haven't seen yet (and would likely never look for yourself). Imagine a news selection algorithm that isn't trying to reinforce what you already believe about the world but instead uses its intelligence to show you the news you most likely haven't been exposed to but would benefit from.

If the thought of Google picking the shoes for you to walk in makes you feel uncomfortable, fair enough. I agree that this would require a level of trust in the tech giants they haven't necessarily earned yet. But what if, instead, you could have full control over whose shoes you would like to walk a mile in today? I would love to see what an extroverted emotionally stable version of myself would see on Instagram—I can only hope it would still involve cat videos.

For all its risks of trapping us in our own echo chambers, psychological targeting could be a real game-changer in how we learn about the world. For the first time in history, we could step out of our shoes and start exploring the world from the viewpoint of someone who is entirely different. Not just any viewpoints, but viewpoints that we define and might never otherwise get to experience.

To be clear, we might not use these different exploration modes all that often. Life in our echo chambers is too comfortable. It feels good to have the world reassure your beliefs and values. In most instances, Google's optimized recommendations are precisely what I want. I want its search engine to know what I'm looking for. Don't dare make me go to page two!

But then there are these rare occasions when I am itching to break out of my comfort zone. To see what the world looks like from a different perspective. The *Roe v. Wade* supreme court case, for example, was one of these occasions. I would have loved to see what the Google's recommended articles looked like for an older male Republican in Texas. Chances are I wouldn't have liked the content very much (just as the guy probably wouldn't have appreciated mine). But I want to at least have the option to see it.

And perhaps psychological targeting could do even more than that. It could help me better understand what I'm seeing. I don't necessarily mean it would help me agree with the opinion of the person whose shoes I'm wearing. It's hard to imagine changing my mind about the importance of a woman's right over her reproductive choices. But I wouldn't want to simply dismiss the person's reality either. Or worse, become so appalled by what I see that I dig my heels in even deeper. That's what got us into the current political mess in the first place.

What we need is a bridge between the different realities we live in. A way to tailor our new shoes to make them fit just a little bit better so that we can continue exploring the unchartered path ahead of us. Think back to what I have told you about Matthew Feinberg and Rob Willer's work on moral reframing in chapter 5. We are far more likely to relate to the arguments of the other side if we get a chance to think them through using our own moral lens. That's what psychological targeting has to offer.

Imagine having a personalized conversation partner who takes the time to sit down with you and helps you digest what you see. Who engages in a real conversation. With all the back and forth, arguments and counterarguments, and questions and answers a true political debate deserves (but without the animosity we might experience when talking to our next-door neighbor).

I'm not talking about another human, but an AI. With language models such as ChatGPT having become increasingly adept at natural conversation, this isn't a far-fetched dream but a reality already. As the psychologist Thomas Costello and his colleagues at MIT have shown, personalized conversations with a GPT-based chatbot reduced people's beliefs in conspiracy theories by about 20 percent. That's a truly remarkable accomplishment considering how hard it is to change people's minds about deeply held beliefs that are core to their identity.[15] And just like we are more likely to confide in Google than our spouse when it comes to questions about sex and money, we might feel more comfortable asking ChatGPT politically charged questions. "I am pro-choice but was shocked to find out that you can detect a fetus's heartbeat as early as six weeks into the pregnancy. Could there be good reasons for a liberal to opposed abortion?" "My family supports the Second Amendment, but I worry about my children at school. What arguments could I use to change their mind?" Having these conversations isn't going to solve the political tribalism problem overnight. But maybe, just maybe, it could lead us back to a more constructive dialogue between people who simply see the world in different ways.

. . .

The three examples offer a sneak peek into how psychological targeting could potentially be a catalyst for social good. But not all of them are a reality yet. Some are mere dreams in need of bold leadership to bring them to life. Others already exist but are yet to realize their full potential. And there are still others I haven't discussed.

Undoubtedly, there's much more work to be done. But it starts with people like you and me daring to ask the *what if* questions. To pause and think about all the ways in which psychological targeting could help people live healthier and happier lives. Individually and collectively.

Leaving my village allowed me to appreciate the benefits of being known to the people around me. I'm grateful for that opportunity.

But while I now view village life more positively in retrospect, it will never be entirely positive. The things I hated about it as a teenager would still frustrate me today. Even though I miss some of the intimacy the village provided, I'm still not keen on people meddling in my life without permission.

The same holds true for psychological targeting. No matter how confident I am that psychological targeting could make the world a better place, I've never been able to shake off my discomfort with it entirely.

And as we will explore in the next chapters, there are good reasons to be skeptical.

7

When Things Go Wrong

In 2020, a woman in the south of China applied to relocate to Hong Kong with her husband, but her request was denied. The reason? An algorithm had flagged their relationship as suspicious. The couple hadn't spent enough time in the same place, and when they failed to celebrate the Spring Festival together, the algorithm sounded the alarms and concluded that the marriage was fake. Cases like this show how your personal data can be used to discriminate against you. However, the latest plans by the Chinese government go far beyond this, and—for the first time—include forms of psychological targeting.

As a recent investigation by the *New York Times* revealed, the Chinese government is rolling out profiling technology that not only tracks its citizens but is increasingly geared toward preventive action.[1] This includes using people's psychological dispositions and current situations (see chapters 2–4) to predict their likelihood of petitioning a government action or participating in a protest. Short-tempered, paranoid, or overly meticulous? High risk of voicing dissent. Even higher risk if you've recently gone through some personal trauma or tragedy. Sorry, but with those statistics, you aren't welcome in Beijing. You could pose a threat to the government, and officials don't like to take chances. Should you try to make your way to the capital anyway, you will be placed under heavy surveillance and potentially stopped.

Psychological targeting opens the door for a whole new level of discrimination that isn't merely based on what we can observe on the surface but what lies beneath. In 2016, Li Wei, a scientist at China's National Police University, described this trend, noting, "Through the application of big data, we paint a picture of people and give them labels with different attributes. For those who receive one or more types of labels, we infer their identities and behavior, and then carry out targeted preemptive security measures."[2]

Are you suffering from mental health problems? Do you have HIV? Or are you an unemployed young adult? In China, any of these labels could mean heavy surveillance and restrictions on the public places you are allowed to visit.

It's possible that you don't find any of this particularly alarming. I teach a class on the ethics of personal data to executives at Columbia Business School. There are always a handful of people who respond to my cautionary tales with a snide comment about how they don't care about their privacy and have given up the idea of ever getting it back.

And I can relate to their sentiment. Trying to reclaim what should be ours by law can feel like an impossible uphill battle. But there are at least two problems with comments like this. First, I don't believe them. Not because I think they are lying to me when they say they don't care, but because I believe that their judgment is based on at least one of the two fallacies that trick our brains into jumping to the wrong conclusion: the "It's worth it" fallacy and the "I have nothing to hide" fallacy (more on those later).

Second, giving up on privacy means giving up on much more than just your right to be left alone. It means giving up on your ability to make your own decisions.

As the philosopher Carissa Véliz puts it in the title of her book: "Privacy is power." The moment others have unrestricted access to your deepest psychological needs, they gain the power to control what you do—and eventually who you are.

Privacy Isn't Dead . . . Yet

In 1999, the CEO of Sun Microsystems, Scott McNealy, famously declared, "You have zero privacy anyway. Get over it."[3] What seemed like a bold claim at the time has evolved into a near-prophetic statement in today's era of big data.

Notably, only a fraction of this is driven by covert surveillance operations like those uncovered by whistleblowers like Edward Snowden. Much of it stems from the everyday choices we make: *we* decide to use Facebook, *we* decide to enable GPS tracking, and *we* decide to invite Alexa into our homes.

Has privacy become obsolete just as McNealy predicted? Even if we aren't as cynical as some of my students, our behaviors seem to suggest so. When was the last time you carefully read the terms and conditions of the products you're using?

But let me ask you this: Would you be comfortable letting a friend or colleague scroll through your messages? What about making your Google searches publicly available? And what about releasing all your credit card transactions and GPS locations?

My guess is that these options don't seem particularly appealing to you. Just think about the offline equivalents of these examples. The postal worker reading your mail, the therapist selling your session transcripts, and the stalker following your every step would all go to jail. If you still think you've lost all appetite for privacy, I encourage you to take down your window blinds and remove all your account passwords. No need for them in your blissful post-privacy existence.

But, if our fundamental need for privacy isn't dead, then why do we do so little to protect it and instead try to convince ourselves we've stopped caring?

Over the years of talking to students and giving public talks, I have come to realize that people often substitute the question whether they care about their privacy with two simpler and misleading ones:

Is sharing my data worth it? and *Am I worried about my data being out there?*

These questions serve as mental shortcuts to a more complex issue—whether we care about our privacy and should be more protective of it. They might seem reasonable substitutes at first glance, but they can lead us astray, masking our true feelings about privacy and influencing our actions in ways that may not serve our best long-term interests.

The "it's worth it" fallacy

When I ask students whether they care about their online privacy and how they protect it, they often respond by reciting all the benefits they would have to give up if they didn't share their personal data. They tell me about Google Maps, Netflix recommendations, and Uber rides.

I wholeheartedly agree that these are fantastic perks. But that's answering a different question: Is sharing my personal data worth it?

Granted, this approach doesn't seem completely unreasonable. We often assess the value of a certain item by how much it would hurt us to give it up. I know that drinking five cups of coffee a day might not be great for my health, but I simply enjoy the experience too much to change my behavior.

Similarly, sharing your personal data can come with amazing benefits that you might simply be unwilling to give up: turn off the GPS on your smartphone and you are lost without Google Maps; disable your social media accounts and you will be disconnected from your social life; cancel your credit card and you might have a hard time getting by.

But just because the benefits of sharing your personal data might outweigh the potential risks doesn't mean you don't care about your privacy (just as me deciding to have five cups of coffee a day doesn't mean that I wouldn't also like to be healthy). All it means is that your immediate desire for pleasure or convenience supersedes your privacy concerns.

Ideally, wouldn't you prefer to enjoy these services while also maintaining a high level of privacy? What makes substituting the original question with a cost-benefits analysis particularly problematic is that we are caught in an unfair battle against the tech industry, which has every incentive to highlight the benefits of sharing our personal data and no incentive to highlight the costs.

The upside of sharing your location data with Google Maps is obvious and immediately tangible. You get to where you want faster without ever getting lost. A no-brainer. The downside of doing so is a lot more nebulous.

Think about it for a second: What exactly are the potential costs of sharing your geo-location with smartphone applications? What are the types of inferences about you that someone can draw from getting access to your longitude and latitude coordinates? And how could this information be used to your detriment, now or in the future?

Before reading this book, you probably had a vague suspicion that sharing your location with third parties could reveal more about you than you might like. It might give away your home address or the place you work. It might reveal which stores you regularly shop in. But I doubt that any of the January 6 rioters at the US Capitol expected their GPS records to get them up to twenty years in jail. And it almost certainly isn't top of mind for most people that our GPS records can offer insights into your personality and mental health.

But there's more. In many instances, you might not even be aware that you're sharing data in the first place.

Take the example of a young woman—let's call her Anna—whose naked picture was posted on social networks without her permission in December 2022.[4] The picture showed her in a lavender shirt sitting on the toilet with her white pants pulled down all the way to her ankles. The mystery wasn't just how the picture had found its way online. Anna had no idea when the picture was taken, let alone who had taken it. How could someone capture such an intimate moment without her knowing? It wasn't a heartbroken ex. Nor the work of a skilled three-year-old toddler. The culprit turned out to be her Roomba vacuum cleaner.

Anna had been part of a customer focus group tasked with testing a new Roomba model. She had signed the paperwork without much thinking, welcoming the fully automated master snooper into her home. The fine print of the agreement stated that the vacuum cleaner could take pictures at any given point in time and that all footage belonged to iRobot.

The purpose of this exercise wasn't to spy on people in precarious bathroom situations. The data was collected to train Roomba's object recognition models to improve its navigation abilities. None of this mattered to Anna. Her naked picture had been leaked by contract workers in Venezuela, and there was nothing she could do to get it back.

The "it's worth it" fallacy focuses our attention on the few occasions in which we happily share our data for better service. But that's the exception, not the rule. In the same way Anna didn't benefit from having her naked picture leaked online, you don't benefit from most of the ways in which your data is used. But because we are constantly reminded of the amazing benefits some of the data-hoarding technologies around us do offer, we don't even think about asking for more.

You shouldn't be forced to choose between convenience and service on the one hand, and privacy on the other (I'll return to this in chapter 9). You should demand and receive both.

The "I have nothing to hide" fallacy

A second response I hear whenever I raise concerns about data privacy is: "I am not worried about my privacy, because I have nothing to hide." This sentiment is a narrative that has been skillfully nurtured by Silicon Valley: if you don't feel comfortable with others accessing your personal data, something must be wrong with you.

But that's nonsense. As the whistleblower Edward Snowden eloquently argued in his book *Permanent Record*, privacy is not about hiding something illegal or shameful. It's about maintaining control over your personal information and having the freedom to decide for yourself how that information is collected, used, and shared.

I believe my students when they say they are not worried about their data being out there. But adopting this mindset is shortsighted and potentially dangerous.

Not having to worry about your personal data getting into the wrong hands is a privilege. Remember how computers can predict sexual orientation from Facebook likes, status updates, and even photographs? Being gay remains a crime in seventy countries around the world. And some countries, including six nations that are members of the United Nations, still impose the death penalty for same-sex sexual activities.

Granted, as tragic as this reality might be for those who suffer from the consequences of a post-privacy world, it might not be immediately obvious why it should impact how *you* personally feel about sharing your data. You might fully empathize with the gay population in Saudi Arabia. But if there is no reason for you to believe that your data could hurt you in any way, why would you be opposed to sharing it? But no matter how safe and comfortable you feel about sharing data right now, you cannot predict what is going to happen with it in the future.

Take the history of my own home country. In 1938, Germany was a democracy. In 1939, it wasn't. Over 6 million Jews from all over Europe lost their lives in the Holocaust. And the accessibility of personal data played a major role in the number of atrocities. Some countries, including the Netherlands, appended official census records with religious affiliation, making it easy for the Nazis to track down and arrest members of the Jewish community. Other countries, including France, did not have this information. In France, about

25 percent of the Jewish population perished. In the Netherlands, 73 percent did.

Now imagine the Nazi regime having access to the digital footprints of every single person in Germany and the rest of Europe. What if they knew exactly what people were doing, where they were going, and who they were socializing with?

The Apples, Facebooks, and Googles of the time might have been happy to share user data with the Nazi regime and secure themselves a spot in the limelight. And even if their CEOs had resisted the pressure to comply, they would have simply been replaced with ones that were more amenable to the intentions of the government. If you are like me, you'd rather not imagine this. The thought sends chills down my spine every single time.

This is precisely why robust privacy and data protection laws are so essential. The risk of a gay person in Saudi Arabia today, or that of a regime-critical citizen in China, could one day be risks you face in your own country.

The 2022 Supreme Court decision to overturn *Roe v. Wade* made this painfully real for American women. Within a matter of days, millions of women suddenly had to worry that their search histories, use of period-tracking apps, online purchases, or GPS location data could be used against them.

No matter how safe and comfortable you feel now, your data could be misused in the future. Always remember: data is permanent, but leadership isn't.

Why Your Life Isn't Truly Yours without Privacy

You might still be skeptical whether privacy is really such a big deal. Maybe you prefer to live in the here and now rather than worry about some hypothetical risk in the future. But here's the catch. By giving away your personal information, you're not just risking a potential future threat. You're sacrificing something valuable and tangible, right now . . . your self-determination.

Giving up your privacy means giving up the freedom to make your own choices and live life on your own terms. When others have access to your personal data and can use it to gain intimate insights into who you are, they hold power over you and your decisions.

Take the case of Kyle Behm, a young man from Maryland. In 2014, Kyle had taken a break from studying at Vanderbilt University to deal with some mental health issues. He was looking for a part-time job when his friend recommended him for a minimum-wage position at a Kroger supermarket. The application seemed like a formality. After all, Kyle was a smart and talented university student. But Kyle was turned down for the job.

Flabbergasted by the outcome, he asked his friend for an explanation. He was told that his application had been "red-lighted" by the personality test he had taken during the interview process. Kyle's honest reporting of his struggles with bipolar mood swings had made his neuroticism score shoot through the roof.

The testing company Kronos put a red flag on his application, raising concerns that Kyle was likely to ignore customers if they were upset. Faced with this prognosis, Kroger rejected his application. As did every other company Kyle applied to; they all used the same personality test.

Kyle had lost control over his life. Others had decided for him that his personality wasn't suited for even the most basic jobs. What was his life going to look like? With all doors being shut in his face, what was he going to do? Desperate and hopeless, Kyle took back control over his life one last time. He committed suicide.

Kyle's tragic story was featured in the 2021 HBO documentary *Persona: The Dark Truth Behind Personality Tests*, which examines the use and impact of personality tests in various parts of society such as the workplace, schools, and even dating. Although the documentary's narrative is one-sided and lacks critical nuance, it drives home an important lesson: the choices we have available to us, and the paths our lives could take, are often shaped by others' perceptions of who we are.

As in my village, these perceptions can both open and close doors for us. My neighbors introduced me to the right people when I needed a job because they thought of me as reliable and trustworthy. However, for the same reasons, they also sometimes forgot to invite me to some of the more questionable—but fun—events going on in the underground scene of Vögisheim (and yes, my dad being a police officer probably didn't help either). In the case of Kyle, the perceptions generated by the personality test closed not just one but many doors.

It gets worse when you move away from self-reported questionnaires to automated personality predictions from people's digital footprints. That's not hypothetical. There are plenty of companies offering just that. TurboHire, for example, deploys chatbots and natural language processing to infer your personality, promising recruiters faster screening of job applicants.

Similar promises are made by Crystal Knows, a company that analyzes publicly available information on websites like LinkedIn to predict a candidate's personality. Such automated assessments strip away every last bit of agency you might have had over the recruiting process.

Despite all the shortcomings of traditional self-reported surveys, you were still in charge of answering the questions. It was up to you how to respond to the question, "Do you make a mess of things?" Once companies start predicting your psychological traits via machine learning algorithms, you have no say in that matter whatsoever.

But that's not even the worst part. Losing control over how other people think of you is never fun. However, it's particularly upsetting when their perceptions are inaccurate. Or plain wrong. Predictive models can be fairly accurate on average and still make plenty of mistakes at the individual level.

To be clear, humans aren't perfect either. Hiring managers don't need test scores or computer-based prediction of personality traits to make discriminating hiring decisions. As humans, we have plenty of stereotypes and decision-making biases to fall back on.

If you're open-minded and extroverted, for example, you are more likely to hire the open-minded extrovert than the more conservative introvert (a phenomenon known as the similarity principle). But even though human biases are often harder to detect and correct for, they are usually less systematic than algorithmic bias.

Think back to Kyle's example. The moment a company used Kronos's assessment as part of its hiring, he was doomed. Kyle's profile was always interpreted the same way: strong agreement with questions $1 + 5 =$ high neuroticism = red flag. While some hiring managers interviewing him might have come to the same conclusion, others might have shown more empathy or used different selection criteria altogether. The job wouldn't have been guaranteed, but it could have at least been an option. A bias in a standardized test or predictive algorithm means game over.

It is tempting to assume that doors close (rather than open) for those unfortunate enough to possess personalities we consider problematic. Kyle's high levels of neuroticism are a prime example. Most of us don't like to admit that our emotions get the best of us sometimes. Is it really so surprising, then, that Kyle had a hard time finding a job? As comforting as this assumption might be, it's not only morally but also factually wrong.

Take agreeableness—the personality trait typically thought of as highly desirable. It's good to be seen as nice and caring, isn't it? Well, that depends on what you're trying to solve for. As I said in the previous chapter, agreeableness is also the trait that has been linked to higher levels of loan defaults. If your bank learns that you are the nice and caring type, it might think twice about offering you a loan. And even if it does, your high-risk disposition might get you terms that are much less favorable than those your more critical and competitive counterparts receive.

But granting others access to your personal data—and with it, your psychology—does not only determine what options are available on your life's menu. It can also influence which options you choose. And we're not talking peanuts here.

You make about 35,000 decisions every day.[5] Those decisions could be as mundane as choosing today's socks or breakfast cereal, or as consequential as deciding which career to pursue or who to marry. Even though we all love the idea of being in control of our decisions, few of the choices we make are entirely our own. We are influenced by what other people do, the context in which a decision is made, or our mental state at the time we make a decision.

Think of the last time you went grocery shopping hungry. Chances are you not only bought more food than you needed, but your cart may have had a few additional items that were more satisfying than healthy.

As I have shown in the previous two chapters, the ability to tap into your psychological needs and motivations gives others power to interfere with your decisions and potentially alter them. In some cases, that might be extremely helpful. But in others, it might not. And in too many instances, you might not even be aware you are being manipulated.

Ever thought about buying life insurance? As a life insurance company, I want to know if you're a little neurotic. If you are, I will add you to my shortlist and make sure to repeatedly target you with offers. Granted, life insurance might be just what you need to put your mind at ease. But even if that's the case, the mere fact that I've singled you out as a potential target and exposed you to many more ads than your emotionally stable neighbor means that you did not make the decision to buy life insurance alone. Or maybe I leverage your anxiety to sell you a little more than you need? Highlighting all the terrible risks you could be facing without life insurance might be enough to get you to reach a little deeper into your pocket.

In contrast to Kyle's story, I'm not creating or wiping out paths your life could have taken. I'm simply making some of the paths more appealing than others. I might not be able to convince you to swerve all the way from the outer right to the outer left path—just as I don't think Cambridge Analytica could have easily converted a die-hard Democrat into a Trump supporter—but many of the paths we can choose from are near one another. No need for a hard swerve; a small and gentle course correction will do. Should I buy Colgate or Crest? Study psychology or economics? Travel to Italy or Croatia?

As I've shown in chapter 5, insights into your psychology give me the instruction manual for how to paint these paths such that you pick the one I want you to travel on. Sometimes, that might not be the end of the world. If I get you to buy Crest toothpaste instead of Colgate, who cares? But what if I aimed to influence which partner you pick, where you invest your money, or who you vote for? Or all of the above? At what point does your life no longer belong to you?

It all comes down to this: you can't take control of your life without privacy. Only when access to your personal data—and with it, the inferences that can be derived from it—is restricted, do you truly have the choice over what to share, with whom, and for what purpose.

You need privacy to be the conductor of your own life.

Haven't We Seen All This Before?

Our history is replete with examples of discrimination and manipulation. While we might not have called it psychological targeting, we naturally try to read the people we encounter, learn about them, and then use that knowledge to decide how to interact. We mingle with the good guys and avoid the bad guys (unless you're a motorbike-loving teenage girl, of course). We recommend movies based on what we believe our friends will enjoy. And we intuitively adapt our speech to suit the listener.

You don't talk to a three-year-old kid the same way you talk to your mom or your boss. When I was young, I knew exactly how to ask my dad for a favor, and how to persuade my mom to give in. These forms of psychological targeting come so naturally to us that we typically don't even notice using them.

What makes the algorithmic version of psychological targeting so different from its traditional counterparts is the mere scale at which it can be deployed. Our face-to-face interactions might be highly personalized, but they are also highly limited in scope. In most cases, personalized conversation is a one-on-one endeavor. Psychological targeting, in contrast, can reach millions of people all at once.

At the same time, there's no reciprocity in the process anymore. Back in the village, my neighbors invaded my privacy, and I invaded theirs. They influenced my decisions, and I returned the favor. Today, it's largely a one-way street with anonymous counterparts pouring money into understanding and changing our minds. And we do not stand the slightest chance to counter their moves.

Importantly, the scalability and unidirectionality of psychological targeting alone don't make it a novel threat. Any radio ad or TV commercial is some sort of large-scale manipulation, and Cambridge Analytica or the Chinese government aren't the first to figure out how to use new broadcast technologies to silence contrarian voices and stir fear among the public either.

However, while the goals of psychological targeting and its traditional counterparts might be similar, there's a big difference. Not only do traditional TV or radio propaganda follow a one-size-fits-all approach, but they are also visible to everybody (that is kind of the point). Psychological targeting, on the other hand, happens entirely in the dark. We have no idea what content and marketing other people receive.

One reason why it took so long to recognize the interference of Cambridge Analytica and other actors in the presidential election was that the ads were targeted. The propaganda was only visible to those with the highest likelihood of following it. And even among those targets, the propaganda seen by one person in Houston, Texas, might have been entirely different from that seen by another person just a few blocks down the road.

It is like being in a dark backstreet with Mark Zuckerberg, who whispers in your ear whatever the highest bidder asks him to. Not exactly a pleasant thought!

The modern version of psychological targeting is so powerful (and therefore potentially dangerous) because it combines two different worlds. It follows the scale of traditional propaganda but has the granularity and depth of face-to-face interactions.

For now, there is no way to collectively monitor what is being said and shared, making controlling this explosive combination a herculean task that we haven't yet learned how to master.

. . .

The tension between the bright and dark sides of psychological targeting in many ways mirrors the tension I experienced in growing up in the village.

Just as being seen and understood allowed me to receive the guidance and support of people who wanted me to succeed in life, psychological targeting can make us all better off—both individually and collectively. But in the same way that my neighbors often interfered with my life in self-serving ways I didn't appreciate, psychological targeting can also be used to exploit our deepest fears and let us dance like mindless marionettes.

As a teenager, I had no choice but to deal with the ups and downs of village life. For me, this meant learning to play the game to my advantage. I found ways to encourage my neighbors' support whenever I needed it. And I got better at protecting myself from their uninvited interference.

We need to do the same for today's digital village. Just as I couldn't simply pack up my things and leave, we can't go back in time to a place where big data and technologies like psychological targeting don't exist. We can't put the genie back in the bottle. But we can become better at managing it.

That's what part 3 of the book is all about.

PART THREE

MAKING OUR DATA WORK FOR US

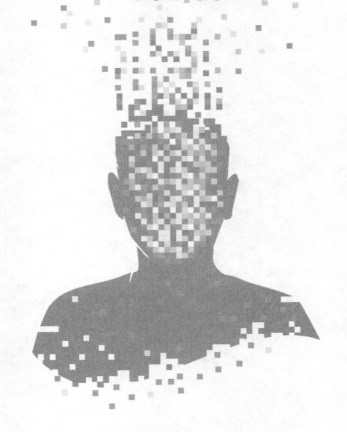

8

We Need More Than Control

I first met Tom in February 2019, about a year after I moved from Cambridge to New York. He had emailed me to discuss a business idea related to psychological targeting. Would I be willing to spare an hour and meet him for lunch near the Columbia campus?

Requests from strangers like Tom aren't unusual. I am often contacted by companies that want to improve the effectiveness of their product recommendations, marketing campaigns, or customer communication. Or by people aiming to establish their own business in that space.

While many of the people I meet genuinely care about improving their customers' experience, it's an open secret that—ultimately—their goal is to make money. Happy customers are loyal customers, after all. And loyal customers are profitable.

A quick search on LinkedIn confirmed my suspicion. Tom was working in investment banking. I immediately dumped him into my mental "Wall Street guy" box and adjusted my expectations accordingly.

But I was wrong. As we sipped coffee, he told me he was planning to leave the world of investment banking. And he was committed to using some of the money he made to make a positive dent on the world.

He could have done that in a million different ways. But he decided to tackle a problem I had been thinking about for a very long time: How do we share some of the value generated by personal data with the people who produce it?

If data is the new oil, can we create an economy that benefits not only those who know how to refine it but everybody?

ApplyMagicSauce

Tom and I spent the next three hours brainstorming what a marketplace like this could look like. The idea itself seemed promising. Shift ownership of data to the individual and facilitate an exchange that creates value for both sides. But we quickly identified a common concern: How would people know how much their data is worth?

Think about it: If all your personal data belonged to you, how much would I have to pay you to get access to your entire Facebook profile? Your GPS records? Your credit card histories? You probably have no idea and will likely aim too low.

It's extremely difficult to understand the value of the digital footprints you generate if you think of them in isolation and don't have any insights into how they could or will be used. Before I started researching psychological targeting, it would have never occurred to me that my banking app could use the location records it collects to predict my mental health and personality (or more likely to sell this data on to someone else to do this). My location data didn't strike me as particularly valuable.

But what if we could show people the real, potential value of their data by giving them access to the same insights that companies like Facebook, Google, and X/Twitter use to turn them into cash cows?

Back at the Cambridge Psychometrics Center, we had tried to do this by building an open-access tool that allowed people to submit their Facebook, X/Twitter, or LinkedIn data and receive predictions of their psychological traits. We called it ApplyMagicSauce and put it on the internet free of charge (it's still there if you want to check it out: applymagicsauce.com).

Tom and I started wondering if we could expand on the idea. We were intrigued by the question whether offering such a self-insights tool could help people appreciate the value of their personal data. Together with Tom's team and two of my colleagues, Adrian Ward and Martin Abel, we set out to study the question.

As an academic used to limited research budgets, I probably would have patched together a small lab experiment using ApplyMagic-Sauce. I would have invited a few Columbia students to the lab, showed them the insights we could glean about their psychology, and asked them a few questions about how much they thought their personal data was worth. But Tom had different plans. As a former Wall Street guy, he wasn't going to play small. He wanted to run the study properly, with real people and a real product.

It took over a year of intense work to build an application that was able to connect to users' Facebook and Google accounts and generate a broad variety of insights we believed would be of interest to people. It showed them their basic sociodemographic profile—name, address, age, gender—and extracted their Google search histories, Facebook likes, and status updates.

But what Tom's team had built wasn't just an app. It was the perfect experimental playground for us to test our hypotheses. Instead of having just one fixed user experience, the app allowed us to compare the impact of different types of "packaging." How would people react if we only showed them the raw data, the way that Facebook and Google are now mandated to do for their users upon request?

You see a small snippet of what this looks like in figure 8-1. Not exactly user friendly, is it? If anything, showing your data this way might make you value it less, not more. I mean, why would anyone pay for this junk?

But what if we helped people sort through the clutter by presenting the information in a more accessible form? A simple bullet-point list? Or perhaps a more elaborate data story? After all, humans are

FIGURE 8-1

Raw data from Google and Facebook

```
"first_name" :  "John"
"last_name" :  "Snow"
"full_name" :  "John Snow"
"age" : "36"
"address" :  "123 Dreamlane"
"hometown" :  "New York, NY"
"zipcode" :  "10001"
"gender" :  "Male"
"recentSearch" :  ["can dogs eat watermelon",
             "how to make nacho salad" ,
             "insomnia treatments",
             "elis winebar uws opening hours"
             "whisky sour ingredients"]
"eventsInterested" : ["michael's bachelor party",
             "burning man",
             "spsp san diego"
```

known to construct their life narratives and identities in the form of stories. Maybe people needed to see their own data story to be able to relate to it.

We ended up testing five different insight variations, ranging from the raw data I showed you in figure 8-1 all the way to an elaborate data story. The latter not only included the information Facebook and Google had captured for each user (e.g., all search queries) but also the types of inferences that could be made based on these data points (e.g., credit scores, political ideology, emotions) and potential use cases (e.g., targeted advertising, personalized pricing of loans).

The final decision we had to make before running the study was how to capture the value that people assigned to their personal data. It's easy to say that you would want at least $50 for your data if the question is purely hypothetical. That's the angel on your shoulder talking, the one with the good intentions ("Richard, we need to protect our privacy").

But what if I offered you and a thousand other people actual money for your data? What if I told you that the fifty people who were willing to accept the least amount would receive the extra cash on the spot in exchange for their data. If you're interested in making some extra cash, you would likely become a bit less ambitious in your demands. At the very least, you would have to think carefully about how much your data is *actually* worth to you. It's the angel in conversation with the devil ("Richard, remember that we need to protect our privacy" versus "Forget about privacy, Richard, we want the money").

That's exactly what we did in the experiment we ran. We first offered people a deal to sell their data on the spot for $10. After that, we asked them for the smallest amount they would be willing to accept in competitive future bids that could only accommodate a limited number of people. This setup allowed us to gauge people's real preferences. The choices they made weren't purely hypothetical. There was real money on the line.

A Dead End

After months of designing the experiment and infrastructure, we were ready to launch. We recruited over 1,500 people online and randomly assigned them to one of the five different insight versions we had (plus a control group of people who didn't see any insights before being asked to sell their data). As with the other big field studies I had run with Hilton and the beauty retailer, I was nervous. We had all invested an enormous amount of time and money in this experiment. I had written the code to analyze the data weeks in advance. I wanted to be ready and be able to see the results immediately.

When I finally got the data from Tom's team, I sat down, opened my code, took a deep breath, and hit "Run." A few seconds later, I could see the results pop up on my screen.

Nothing.

Although 75 percent of our participants said they were concerned or very concerned about data privacy, most of them sold their data anyway (85 percent on average). Worse, there were no differences across the various insight conditions we had worked so hard on. It didn't matter if someone saw the raw data in junk format, the bullet points, or the full-on data story. They were all equally likely to sell their data and asked for roughly the same amount of money in future iterations. Not only that, people who saw their data in one form or another were just as likely to sell their data as the people in the control group who were asked to sell their data without seeing any of the insights.

To say I was disappointed would be an understatement. A massive understatement. It's the kind of outcome you dread as a scientist after having spent hundreds of hours and thousands of dollars on an experiment. It felt like an utter failure. I informed the entire team about the results and buried my head in the sand for a few days.

But then something in my thinking changed. I guess that's what happens when you see the world from a different perspective (upside down, engulfed in darkness, that is). The experiment had failed to produce the results we were hoping to see. But it had still taught us an important lesson (sometimes, no effect *is* indeed a finding, even if we don't like it).

Pulling back the curtain and educating people about the insights third parties could derive from their data wasn't enough to change their behavior. We had equipped people's angels with better tactical knowledge and weapons. And yet, they stood no chance against the devil's immediate cash reward.

Toward a Better Solution

This simple insight turned out to be a real epiphany that made me reconsider one of the main solutions I had previously advocated for.

I had been a strong supporter of new data protection regulations like the General Data Protection Regulations in Europe or the California Consumer Protection Act in the state of California. Both regulations are aimed at empowering consumers by mandating high levels of transparency and control.

Empowering consumers has a lot of appeal and in many ways seems like the ideal solution. It's not only a morally defensible solution, but also allows us to make the most of our personal data. We all feel differently about disclosing personal information and how much we value the services that rely on our data. You might be comfortable sharing your GPS location to get relevant weather updates. I might not. Instead of imposing crippling one-size-fits-no-one regulations, let us decide. At the end of the day, it's our data, so why shouldn't we be the ones choosing when and how we want to share it?

Don't get me wrong. Transparency and control are critical for helping us navigate the tension between the potential harms and benefits of sharing our personal data. And I certainly support the intention behind these new regulations and the fundamental values they represent. But as our failed experiment with Tom suggested, transparency and control alone are often insufficient to help people make the right decisions.

The more I thought about this, the more disheartened I felt. It struck me that in the current data ecosystem, control is far less of a right than it is a responsibility—one that most of us are not equipped to take on. What we get is control without mastery.

Left to our own devices, most of us fail rather spectacularly when it comes to making informed privacy decisions. Our good intentions rarely translate into behavior—a well-established phenomenon known as the privacy paradox. Most of us say we care about our privacy but do little to protect it (just like the people in our experiment). Think you're the exception? Let me ask you this: When was the last time you updated your privacy settings or carefully read through the terms and conditions before installing an app on your phone? I honestly don't remember when I did.

But even if we got more people to pay attention to privacy policies, there's no guarantee they would arrive at the right conclusions. In a survey administered by the legal scholar Chris Hoofnagle at the University of California, Berkeley, 62 percent of respondents erroneously believed that companies posting privacy policies on their website implied that they could not share their personal data with third parties.[1] Sadly, there's often no incentive for companies to change any of that. The less you care and comprehend, the better.

But why do we have such a hard time managing our personal data responsibly? According to the psychologist Azim Shariff, the answer is quite simple.[2] Our brains simply haven't evolved to solve today's privacy puzzles.

Technology moves at light speed. Evolution doesn't. The privacy challenges we face today are an entirely new species.[3] They have little resemblance to those my grandmother faced even eighty years ago, let alone those our ancestors encountered a century or two back. New technologies have radically altered the privacy landscape over the past few decades. Yet, our brain's cognitive abilities are essentially the same as two thousand years ago.

In chapter 7, I discussed two common fallacies. Many of us substitute the question whether we care about our privacy with the easier—but different—question whether sharing our personal data is worth it (typically without understanding the potential costs of doing so). And we erroneously conclude that just because we feel like we have nothing to hide or worry about, this makes sharing our data safe. That might be true today, but it might not be true tomorrow.

Add to this a general lack of digital literacy a heap of uncertainty around what companies might be doing with your data. I work on these topics full time and still find it impossible to keep up. Unless you are an even bigger tech nerd or privacy activist than me, the data landscape is simply too complex to navigate on your own. In most cases, data collection is an invisible process that happens behind the scenes and that—often by design—remains opaque to those whose data is being collected. Companies know what data they are harvesting, what they do with it, and how much it is worth to them. But you don't.

For thousands of years, the most effective strategy to deal with situations of uncertainty was to look to others for guidance. If many other people followed a certain path or held a certain belief, it paid off to do the same. Privacy was no exception.

While growing up in Vögisheim, many of my early strategies for deciding what to disclose about myself and how to protect my personal life from the curious eyes of my neighbors were borrowed from what I observed in my friends and parents. Most of us do the same in today's digital village. We don't know how to deal with our personal data, so we look to others. Others, who in many cases are just as clueless as we are, and whose behaviors and beliefs are as easily swayed by those who want us to divulge as ours.

Let's imagine our brains magically caught up. That would be fantastic, but still not enough. Managing our personal data would remain a full-time job. You simply don't have the time to carefully read and decipher the legalese of all the terms and conditions you sign off on. Even the most efficient and diligent person only has twenty-four hours in a day. And (hopefully) better things to do than sifting through the terms and conditions of *all* the services and products they use. If you had to choose between sharing a meal with your family or deleting the browsing history on all your devices, which one would you pick?

The bottom line is that we cannot reasonably be expected to handle the responsibility that comes with the right to control our own personal data all by ourselves. Not in the current data ecosystem. There are simply too many forces working against us in this game.

Does all this mean we should give up on transparency and control altogether? Of course not. Tools like the original version of Tom's app should exist for people to see what their data reveals about them.

And you should absolutely have control. It's *your* data after all. But for us to be able to exercise control over the data successfully, we need to create systems that allow us to benefit from this right.

The Perfect Storm

Think of it this way: being the captain of a sailboat is easy and fun when you are drifting along the Mediterranean coast on a sunny day. You can choose any little town to visit. The one with the medieval cathedral or the one with the famous ice cream shop. There are no wrong choices. Now, imagine sailing the same boat through a raging thunderstorm. All by yourself. You could be thrown in any direction. There are twenty emergencies competing for your attention. Steering your boat under these circumstances doesn't feel like a right at all.

Yet, that's exactly what we do. We drop people in the middle of a raging technology storm—alone—and bless them with the right to control their personal data. That simply can't be the optimal solution. We need more than transparency and control. We need to tame the sea with better regulation and staff our boat with a competent crew.

I'm going to start with the first part: How do we tame the sea and create an ecosystem that allows individuals to choose from a bright variety of desirable outcomes, rather than a dark mix of undesirable ones?

9

Creating a Better Data Ecosystem

D esigning an ecosystem that enables people to make smarter decisions about their personal data is a hell of a difficult task. That's not just because the current landscape is complex, but also because it keeps changing at an ever-increasing pace.

Take speech recognition, for example. For years, progress in the ability of machines to understand and produce spoken (and written) language had been stagnating. Technologies like Siri or customer service chatbots were able to parse simple language and have semi-meaningful conversations based on predefined decision trees. But they were far from having a natural free-flowing conversation. And, as I'm sure you will remember fondly, they made mistakes all the time (No, it's M-A-T-Z, not Metz. And no, I don't want to rebook my flight. Main menu. MAIN MENU. Goddamn it, get me on the phone with a real person, RIGHT NOW!).

Until recently, any five-year-old could have easily beaten even the most sophisticated speech-recognition technology. But all of this changed practically overnight in the early 2020s when transformer models hit the market (think: ChatGPT, which was introduced in late 2022). Today, an algorithm can pass tests that require what psychologists refer to as theory of mind. It understands that different protagonists in a story can have different knowledge and different beliefs about the world. And it has conversations that often seem just as natural and personal as those we have with our analog friends.

The fact that technology is changing at light speed means that any sustainable attempt at creating a more supportive ecosystem needs to be able to dynamically adapt to new technological realities. The solutions I outline next are therefore based on broad principles rather than specific implementation strategies. They offer a starting point for policy makers and other benevolent players in the field to reimagine the collection and use of personal data. And they equip you with a list of things to demand from business leaders and regulators.

At the most basic level, I think of this as creating the right channels for desired behavior (borrowed from the "architecture" metaphor in behavioral economics). You want to make it easy for people to protect their personal data and with it their privacy and self-determination. And you want to make it difficult for companies and nefarious actors to abuse your data and manipulate you.

That might sound obvious. But, from our perspective as data producers, the current landscape operates in a "buy high, sell low" manner. It's increasingly difficult (if not impossible) to manage our personal data wisely, while it remains easy for companies and other third parties to take advantage of us. If we want to enjoy our right to control our data, we need to change that.

Here's what this could look like in practice.

Opening the Right Channels

Remember Tom from the previous chapter? After our failed experiment, Tom shifted gears and started to tackle the problem from a different angle. Instead of trying to educate people about the value of their personal data (and help them sell it for a fair price), he created an easy way for them to delete it.

But wait, isn't that counterproductive to helping people benefit from their own data? Deleting a precious resource doesn't create value. If anything, it seems to destroy it. Wrong. Deleting your personal data only puts you at a disadvantage if you are the only one holding a copy. Which couldn't be further from the truth. In most instances, you don't hold a copy of the data yourself. Yet, there are hundreds of entities trading your assets without your consent or knowledge (i.e., the companies collecting your data, or secondhand data brokers).

The fewer people who have access to your data, the more valuable it becomes. For example, you will have a hard time getting a fair price for your personal data when there are twenty other entities selling it for a bargain. Taking control over your data means limiting access to it.

Under some of the world's more progressive data protection regulations—including the General Data Protection Regulations in Europe or the California Consumer Privacy Act—you have the right to request third parties to do just that: delete your personal data. This is a great idea—in principle.

When I started writing this chapter, I reached out to twenty of my friends in Europe and California to ask them whether they had ever requested their personal data to be deleted (and if yes, how often). Take an educated guess how many of my friends had done so (note, there are more than just one or two privacy scholars among them— and many of them have had to endure me rant about data privacy for years now). The answer: zero. Not a single person had used their right to protect their personal data from being traded.

I don't blame them. I haven't either (even though I know very well that I should). It's a classic example of what my friend Dan Ariely, the behavioral economist, calls the space rocket principle of behavior change. To be successful in following through with our intentions, we need two things.

The first one is thrust. People need to be motivated and eager to change. That's what Tom and I had tried to do when we showed participants how intimate—and therefore valuable—their data really was. But as we learned the hard way, motivation alone wasn't enough.

People said they were concerned, but then went ahead and sold their data anyway.

That's where the second factor comes in. To launch a rocket into space, you also need to reduce friction. Making smart decisions about your personal data needs to be seamless. You can't expect people to (e)mail out hundreds of data-deletion requests and (ideally) follow up on every one of them to check for compliance. Limiting third-party access to our personal data needs to be easy.

In Tom's new application, mePrism, which I'm involved in as a science adviser, "easy" means being able to delete your personal data from the servers of hundreds of data brokers with just a few clicks (and an automatic deletion request should the data resurface). A great start, and certainly a significant improvement over the current status quo.

But in an ideal world, easy would mean protecting your privacy without you having to do anything at all. It's what scholars have termed *privacy by design*.

There are numerous ways to put the privacy-by-design principle into practice. I've selected two broad approaches that I believe are not only impactful and relatively easy to apply, but also able to dynamically adjust to the rapid changes in the digital landscape.

First, we need to design systems that use our evolutionary shortcomings to our advantage.

Second, we need to leverage technologies that eliminate the trade-off between privacy and self-determination versus convenience and service.

Turning your inertia into a superpower

In the United States, about twenty people die every day waiting for an organ transplant. Over a hundred thousand people are currently on the waiting list, desperately hoping to receive a donation to save their lives.

A comparison of organ donation registration rates across countries offers intriguing insights into how inertia can be turned from kryptonite into a superpower. Some countries, such as Germany or the United States, require people to register as donors. In the United States, this means filling in an online form for about five to ten minutes, heading to the department of motor vehicles, or mailing in a letter. Other countries, such as Austria or the United Kingdom, register all citizens by default. You can take your name off the registry anytime, but unless you actively unsubscribe, you are part of the club.

Which of these countries do you think have higher rates of organ donors? The countries where people have to register (opt in) or the countries where they get registered by default but can opt out? Yes, it's the opt-out countries. You're much more likely to stay registered than register yourself.

But now try to be a bit more specific with your guess. How big is the difference between the opt-in and opt-out countries. What percentage of the population actively decides to register to become an organ donor in the opt-in countries? 70 percent? 50 percent? 30 percent?

On average, the number is a rather disappointing 15 percent. Even though more than 90 percent support organ donations in national surveys, only fifteen in every one hundred people decide to take the necessary steps to become a potential organ donor themselves.[1]

Now what about the opt-out countries? What percentage of the population do you think decides to stay registered as an organ donor rather than requesting to leave the system? Typically, more than 95 percent! To me, this difference is mind-blowing. It's literally the difference between life and death. Importantly, none of the countries force their citizens to be organ donors. At the end of the day, it's their choice. All they do is change the default and reap the power of our inertia.

Just like the organ donation registries, privacy policies come with a default. And this default—surprise, surprise—typically favors self-disclosure. If you don't want companies to collect all the personal data they can legally access, you have to take action and opt out. That's like designing your privacy spaceship in the shape of an inverted umbrella. Even the most powerful engine will never get you off the ground with that much friction.

The most obvious solution to this problem is to change the default. Require people to opt in rather than opt out. This shift not only makes it easy for people to protect their privacy, but could also indirectly impact people's motivation by increasing the perceived value of their data. How? Through another human kryptonite turned superpower: A well-established decision-making bias called *the endowment effect*.

The basic principle of the endowment effect is captured in the famous Aristotle quote: "For most things are differently valued by those who have them and by those who wish to get them: what belongs to us, and what we give away, always seems very precious to us."[2]

In the context of privacy, the endowment effect causes people to value their privacy more when they already possess it and face the possibility of losing it, compared to when they lack it but have the opportunity to gain it.

In a clever experiment led by economist Alessandro Acquisti at Carnegie Mellon University, research assistants approached unwitting shoppers in a mall and asked them to participate in a short survey in return for a gift card.[3] Here comes the experimental twist: those who agreed to complete the survey were randomly assigned one of two gift cards. The first gift card, worth $10, guaranteed full anonymity. The second, worth $12, was linked to participants' personal information. They were then offered the option to switch their card for the other.

Among those who were originally assigned the less valuable but anonymous card, about half the individuals (52.1 percent) decided to keep their card rather than switching to the traceable, higher-value card. In contrast, only one in ten individuals (9.7 percent) who had originally received the higher-value card decided to switch to the anonymous, lower-value card. That's a huge gap. When we have privacy, we are reluctant to relinquish it. But when we lack privacy, we might be willing to forgo it.

Changing the default for sharing personal data is an important step in the right direction (especially in the absence of better alternatives). But it's not a silver bullet. There are at least two problems with how the principle is currently implemented.

First, most of us have little to no idea what we're agreeing to when we check the "Yes I do" box. Often, the process of informed consent is more akin to the Las Vegas version of a wedding than anything else. You might not think through the consequences of your decision; it just seems like a great idea in the moment.

Maybe you said yes because you were really excited about a certain product but couldn't use it without agreeing to the terms and conditions. Or maybe you simply didn't want to lose any time digging deep into the fine print before accessing the service (think of the last time you accepted all cookies on a website just to get to the content you really wanted to see).

Similar to a typical Las Vegas wedding, we sign all the required paperwork for our decision to qualify as informed consent. But do we really know what we're agreeing to?

Second, changing the default from opt out to opt in requires you to give up convenience and service for privacy and self-determination. For instance, without sharing your location data, you can't use Google Maps to navigate from A to B. And without allowing Siri to listen, voice recognition becomes unavailable.

We should not have to contemplate the value of letting companies use our personal data in this way. In an ideal world, you shouldn't be forced into this trade-off. Instead of an either-or choice, it should be a both-and offer. Privacy *and* service. This might sound like a great idea in theory and impossible in practice, but it isn't.

The technological path to having it all

Back in the village, my neighbors had to observe my behavior to be helpful. And there was no way to prevent them from gaining access to the intricate details of my life if I wanted their support. And once they'd been helpful, I couldn't just go back and ask them to forget what they knew. In any case, I doubt any of them would have shown much interest in that proposition. They enjoyed the gossip.

That requirement no longer holds true in the digital world. We now have technologies that allow your data to remain in its safe harbor while still generating the insights you are looking for. It's as if your neighbor were lending you their brain and resources for a day to process all your problems, without storing any of the data itself (well, kind of).

Sounds like magic, right? It definitely felt like it when I first heard about it. It's math magic called *federated learning*.[4]

The truth is, you don't need to hand over all your data to a third party to get personalized recommendations and convenient services tailored to you. We all carry mini supercomputers in our pockets. Remember the historic *Apollo 11* mission that landed the first man on the moon? Your iPhone today has over 100,000 times more processing power than the *Apollo 11* computer. It has over 1 million times more memory, and over 7 million times more storage.

Federated learning taps into this computing power to run algorithms (and insights) locally. Take Netflix. Instead of sending your viewing data to a central server it owns, Netflix could send its recommendation model to your device (i.e., to your laptop or smartphone, for example). The model would then update itself based on your data and recommend the best shows and movies for you. To make sure we all benefit from this learning, your device would send an encrypted version of the updated model back to Netflix.

The result? You benefit, Netflix benefits, and all the other users benefit. But your personal data never leaves its safe harbor. You don't need to trust a third party (regardless of how trustworthy that party might be) to securely store your data and use it for only the purposes it was intended. Federated learning replaces the need to trust with a system that is inherently trustworthy.

This might sound like science fiction, but it's not. Chances are you're already benefiting from federated learning technology. Apple's

Siri, for example, is trained locally on your device. Using federated learning, Apple can send copies of its speech-recognition models to your iPhone or iPad, where it will process your audio data locally. This means that none of your voice recordings ever need to leave your phone, but Siri still gets better at understanding your needs. Because your phone sends back the updated model to Apple to integrate the new insights into its master model, you are helping to improve the experience of other users.

Governments could mandate technologies like federated learning for companies that have reached a certain number of users or that handle sensitive data. But using such technologies might also be in the best interest of companies. Hoarding large amounts of personal data has become a growing security risk that can be incredibly costly. You don't want to sit on a pile of gold if you know there are robbers lurking all around you waiting for their opportunity to steal it. You'd much rather keep it somewhere safe. Use it to do your business without the mandate to protect it. The same is true for personal data.

Importantly, the shift to privacy by design could also significantly improve the products and services we use. This might seem counterintuitive. Less data should mean lower quality, shouldn't it? It's the classic argument you hear from tech companies. But privacy by design doesn't mean no data. It means trading data in exchange for better service and products. Today, much of this exchange amounts to mere lip service. There is no incentive for companies to fulfill their promises once they've acquired your data, leaving you in a bad position at the bargaining table.

But if companies depended on their customers' active consent to collect and use personal data, they would be compelled to deliver value in return. The formula is simple: no value, no data. Vague promises would no longer suffice. If you don't perceive a benefit from sharing your personal data, you simply wouldn't share it and would move on to another service that does a better job.

Take Instagram. The app's recommendation algorithms promise to deliver the most relevant and engaging content by tapping into users' personal data. That sounds helpful, but how can I be sure it's actually true? Currently, I have to take Instagram's word for it. There is no way for me to compare my personalized feed to a more generic version of the app or one that is based on only a subset of my data that I might feel comfortable sharing.

Once we shift the default to opt in, that changes. The generic version of the app would become my new baseline. For me to change the default, Instagram would need to show me how sharing my personal data gives me a much better experience. If it fails to do so, I could simply revoke data access and either go back to the generic version or move to a competitor that keeps it promises.

Privacy by design empowers us all to ask for more.

Closing the Wrong Channels

Considering the obvious benefits of personal data for the global economy, it's hardly surprising that it is often compared to valuable resources such as oil or gold, an analogy that makes the collection and processing of such data an attractive endeavor. If you stumbled on an oil field or gold mine in your backyard, wouldn't you start mining?

In a 2008 *Guardian* article, the journalist Cory Doctorow offered a different analogy, comparing personal data to nuclear waste. He wrote, "We should treat personal electronic data with the same care and respect as weapons-grade plutonium—it is dangerous, long-lasting and once it has leaked there's no getting it back."[5] Doctorow is right. In the worst case, personal data—just like radioactive material—can be deadly. Literally.

On July 19, 2020, US District Judge Esther Salas and her husband Mark celebrated the twentieth birthday of their son Daniel in their home in New Jersey. The celebration turned into tragedy when a man, posing as a FedEx delivery man, entered their home and opened fire. Salas's son Daniel died on the scene. Her husband, Mark, was critically wounded. The killer, former attorney Roy Den Hollander, had collected personal information about the judge online and assembled what Salas referred to as "a complete dossier on me and my family."[6]

But Doctorow's analogy goes beyond emphasizing the potential harm associated with the collection and use of personal data. While radioactive material can cause unparalleled destruction when weaponized, it also remains one of the cleanest, cheapest, and most reliable sources of energy. Plutonium doesn't care what we do with it, just as personal data doesn't care if it is used to hurt or help people. That decision is up to us.

With nuclear power, the world collectively agreed that the stakes are too high for these decisions to be made without strict regulations. Rather than allowing unrestricted use or banning it entirely, we decided to heavily regulate and control the acquisition, possession, and use of radioactive materials both nationally and internationally. You can't just walk into Walmart and order a pound of plutonium or uranium.

We need to put similar safeguards in place when it comes to personal data and psychological targeting.

The tragedy of Judge Salas and her family led President Joe Biden to pass the Daniel Anderl Judicial Security and Privacy Act in December 2022.[7] The legislation states that "it shall be unlawful for a data broker to knowingly sell, license, trade for consideration, or purchase covered information of an at-risk individual or immediate family." Seeing policy makers acknowledge the potential dangers of personal data makes me optimistic about the future. It's a first step in rewriting the data narrative.

At the same time, however, the new act raises an important question: If we believe it is necessary to protect judges from the potential harm caused by personal data, why doesn't the same principle apply to the rest of us? We might not all be potential targets of hate crimes, but we are all vulnerable to the dangers posed by personal data.

How do we create a system with collective guardrails that—like those introduced in response to the discovery of nuclear power—turn the use of personal data into a force for good rather than bad?

First, we need to impose a cost on the collection and use of personal data, and we need to prevent any one entity from collecting too much radioactive material to (un)intentionally elevate their arsenal to weapons grade.

Companies should face trade-offs, too

While navigating the digital landscape means weighing the costs and benefits of sharing personal data for users, the scenario is different for companies. There's a lot of upside to collecting personal data. It can be used to better understand customers' needs, create better products, or sell for profit to third parties. The incentives are clear: data is a resource that holds enormous economic value.

Yet, there's very little downside for the companies themselves. Back in the village, there was an implicit cost associated with collecting intel on your neighbors. I had to buy my friend a beer to hear the latest gossip. Or I had to make the exchange reciprocal: if my friend shared some gossip, I'd share mine. With the shift to anonymous online exchanges, this is no longer the case. Setting up data dragnets is easy. Storage is cheap.

With a lot of upside and virtually no downside (other than the typically neglected security risks), why wouldn't companies collect our personal data? From a purely economic perspective, it seems foolish not to. It's like ignoring a pile of cash sitting in front of you and saying, "No thanks."

We need to change the immediate incentive structure for companies in a way that introduces trade-offs. Companies should pay a price for collecting personal data, just like you and I pay a price for sharing it.

One potential approach is to tax companies for the collection of personal data, forcing them to reconsider whether they truly need it. Let's take data brokers, for example. These are companies that benefit from your personal data without giving you anything in return—

the type that is targeted by the Daniel Anderl Judicial Security and Privacy Act. They collect as much of your personal data as possible and sell it at a profit to other companies. They're like the old lady in the village who becomes the go-to hub for gossip. She has no interest in using rumors to your advantage or disadvantage. But she enables those who do. The same is true for data brokers. They might not interfere with your life directly. But they are all too happy to support others in doing so.

Imagine a small tax of 2 percent on this industry, which generated about $250 billion—equivalent to the revenue of all US airlines or the GDP of Bangladesh. Imposing a cost on data brokers would not only create a financial disincentive but also generate an additional $5 billion in taxpayer revenue overnight. This money could be used to lower taxes elsewhere or dedicated to the development of privacy-preserving technologies.

Prevent players from collecting all the pieces in our data puzzle

I showed you how different types of digital footprints can be used to make predictions about your most intimate traits. Each of these traces provides a part of the puzzle.

Your Facebook likes to offer insights into how you want to present yourself to others. Your Google searches provide a glimpse into the burning questions that are currently on your mind. And your location data helps me better understand your daily routines. Like a puzzle piece, each data point captures part of you but is incomplete on its own.

The more data points companies can access and combine, the clearer the picture of who you are and what you want becomes. This is what Roger McNamee, an early investor in Facebook (and now avid critic of the company), refers to as "McNamee's seventh law": datasets become geometrically more valuable when you combine them.[8]

Just as the danger of radioactive material increases with mass, so does the danger of personal data. While having a random weather app access my GPS records is concerning, it pales in comparison to big tech companies having access to almost all parts of my data puzzle.

Just think about how many different aspects of your life Google products touch on. There's YouTube, Gmail, Google search, Maps, Chrome, Drive, Calendar, Fit, Play, and so on. Since Google seemingly had a product for every single letter in the alphabet, it's collecting most of our puzzle pieces. And whatever data it doesn't collect itself, it buys.

But what makes the tech giants so dangerous isn't just the mere amount and granularity of data it hoards but its reach. As the saying goes: "You can fool some of the people all of the time, and all of the people some of the time, but you cannot fool all of the people all of the time." If Google tried, it could fool (almost) all the people all the time. That's a dangerous gamble.

How do we prevent any one player from collecting all your digital puzzle pieces? The most obvious starting point is to break up the tech giants into separate corporations that are not allowed to share the same user base, data, or resources (e.g., Gmail, Maps, DoubleClick, and YouTube). This could be achieved with the help of antitrust laws.

I'm not the first to suggest this radical step. Over the last decade, the digital economy has turned into a winner-takes-all arena, with a small number of companies controlling large parts of the market. They control the attention of customers, recruit the brightest talent, and have an enormous influence on lawmakers in Washington. It doesn't take much imagination to see how the mere size, power, and mostly unregulated conduct of the tech giants—Facebook, Alphabet, Amazon, Apple, and Microsoft—makes them top contenders for antitrust regulation.

Although antitrust laws are designed to create and maintain healthy competition, they could also help address privacy concerns they weren't originally designed for. Breaking up the tech conglomerates would not only prevent companies from obtaining access to the full puzzle of your psychology but also reduce the risks associated with data breaches. Right now, a hack of the Google databases might expose not just your emails, but also your searches, your YouTube playlists, and your location data.

Think of it as a central safe in which you store your entire life savings. Even with state-of-the-art protection, there's always a risk that someone could crack it open. Now imagine you had multiple safes, with multiple passwords in multiple locations, all independent of one another. If a thief managed to access one, their haul would be limited to whatever is stored in that particular safe at that particular time.

The main argument against breaking up the tech monopolies is that it would stifle innovation and destroy the value these companies create for their users, shareholders, and the tech ecosystem at large. It is hard to discern whether this concern is genuine or just a convenient excuse for those who benefit from maintaining the current status quo. As the saying goes: "Prediction is very difficult, especially if it's about the future." We can't foresee the future, but we can learn from the past.

In 1982, the government decided to break up Bell Systems. In 1984, AT&T followed. Both times, those opposed to the breakup raised similar concerns to what you hear today in the context of the tech giants. Yet, both times, the decision to invoke antitrust laws created winners all around. It benefited consumers and the broader economy by accelerating innovation and creating a thriving, expanded ecosystem (now Silicon Valley). At the same time, it also generated enormous value for the shareholders of Bell Systems and AT&T.

We can't be certain that the same outcomes would apply to today's tech giants, of course. But as leading voices in the call for antitrust regulation—like Scott Galloway or Tim Wu—have convincingly argued, it very well might. Amazon Web Services, for example, could become one of the biggest success stories in history if broken off from the retail business of Amazon, and Instagram is likely to continue to yield high revenue even if it were no longer part of Meta.

We Can (and Need to) Do More

Redesigning the current data landscape according to the principles I outlined could have a tremendous impact on how we interact with and benefit from our personal data. It would help us establish ground rules that rebalance the highly skewed playing field we've long struggled with.

However, as much as I support systemic changes through regulation and new forms of data management, I believe more is needed.

Taming the sea takes time. New data policies, for example, can create new incentive structures for companies, but they are also extremely slow to pass and difficult to enforce. And even if we managed to calm the waters for a while, we don't know when the next storm will arise. Tomorrow, a new technology might hit the market that changes everything.

But it's not just that. Systemic changes mandated through regulations are typically focused on managing risks for the collective. Introducing a new data tax or enforcing opt-out policies is likely to protect us from the most serious harm. But neither of these two approaches necessarily helps you and me individually when it comes to maximizing the value each of us can extract from our personal data. We might have very different preferences and goals, and each of us may wish to leverage our data in entirely different ways.

What we need is to supplant systemic approaches with a system that provides immediate, flexible support. In other words, we need a competent and trustworthy crew. A crew that works together like a well-oiled machine. One that has the same destination in mind, cares deeply about the well-being of all passengers, and can safely navigate the boat (even when the sea is rough). That's what the final chapter of the book is all about.

10

Coming Together

et's revisit Vögisheim, the quaint village in the southwest corner of Germany where our journey (and my life) began. Many locals and visitors call it the Tuscany of Germany. My Italian friends might consider this a bit of an insult, but the region does bear some resemblance to the birthplace of the Italian Renaissance. Rolling hills and vineyards as far as the eye can see. Rows and rows of grapevines dividing the hills into symmetrical parcels. The regions' wines aren't as well-known as Chianti or Sangiovese, but if you are a wine connoisseur, you might recognize our Gutedel or Spätburgunder.

When I was growing up, my parents still owned vineyards, even though my grandma's family gave up farming in the late 1950s. Every fall, around mid-September, we harvested.

Harvest season was fun (at least for the kids). Armed with big grape hoppers (large backpacks used to carry the grapes) and a sharp pair of garden scissors, we'd walk up and down the rows of vines, snipping and tossing grapes over our shoulders into the hopper. Once filled, we'd empty them into a trailer hitched to a tractor.

As kids, we probably did that for five minutes to feel important before we ran off to play in the fields, watching the adults labor away. At lunch everybody would sit together and eat homemade bread, cheese, and cold cuts. I should say that this entire experience became a lot less romantic once we were teenagers and expected to pull our weight.

Whenever I'm back home, I go for a walk in the vineyards—no matter the weather. One time, I brought a friend visiting from Japan. We walked through my family's vineyards, and I told him about my childhood adventures. He wanted to try our wine. I can imagine you might too.

I had to giggle a little. Our vineyards are far too small to produce our own wine. We neither had the equipment nor the expertise to do so. But, looking back, his question was a good one. He wanted to know, "What happens to the grapes?"

Selling the grapes to one of the big wineries in the area could have been a possibility. But we never harvested enough for this to be a real option. Even if we did, any deal would have greatly favored the winery. So instead of simply letting the grapes go to waste, most families in Vögisheim and the surrounding villages were part of a *Winzergenossenschaft*. Yes, a true beauty of a German word. The English translation is *winemakers' co-op*.

After harvesting the grapes, we dropped them off at the co-op. The co-op would either turn them into wine or sell them to the wineries.

Working with these co-ops had several advantages. First, combining the grapes increased the value of each individual harvest. Second, the co-op brought expertise, both because many of the members were winemakers and because we could pool our resources. The proceeds from the wine and grape sales allowed the co-op to buy advanced equipment, hire expert oenologists to improve the quality of the wine, and bring on marketing professionals to sell it. More than any one of us could have pulled off alone. Pooling our grapes made all of us better off.

The same is true of your personal data. Your individual data isn't worth very much. It only becomes valuable when combined with the data of others. Think of medical research. Your medical record alone won't tell us anything about the risk factors associated with a certain disease. We can only start exploring these factors once we have a sufficiently large pool of carriers (and noncarriers).

The same is true for your Facebook and Google data. The two companies only care about your data because they can connect and compare it to the data of millions of people. That's what allows them to extract the insights third parties are willing to pay for.

But it's not just the value of your data that increases when you pool it with others. Just as my family didn't have the expertise to turn our grapes into wine, most of us don't have the expertise to make good decisions regarding our data (see chapter 8). Left to our own devices, we simply don't stand a chance. We have neither the expertise nor the time. Could my parents have figured out how to make wine? Probably, even though it might not have been very good. But were they eager to dedicate their whole lives to this? Hell no.

Just as the people in my village came together to reap the fruits of their labor, we need to come together in small communities of like-minded people to collectively manage our data and benefit from it. Like wine co-ops, data co-ops are member-owned organizations that pool and manage their members' personal data to benefit the collective. However, unlike wine co-ops, data co-ops don't require people to be in the same place—although they could. Instead, the members can be connected by a common goal and a shared strategy for leveraging their data to accomplish that goal.

Digital Data Villages

Let me give you an example of how a data co-op could work.

As I started writing this book, I got pregnant. A beautiful but also terrifying experience. You get advice from all directions. Do this. Do that. Most of the advice will at some point contradict prior advice you've gotten. Eating sushi might put the baby at risk. No, that's not true. What you must look out for is caffeine. You have access to doctor check-ins every two to four weeks. But what you really want is a minute-by-minute update on how things are going, and the assurance that everything is fine. All this uncertainty drove me nuts.

Now, imagine expectant mothers from around the world sharing their genetic and biometric data, alongside information about their own health and the health of the baby. You could stop the guessing game, and instead base your decisions on actual data. To start with, you could build advanced predictive models to identify general risk factors. Some of them might be known already, but some of them might be new.

Not just that, the members of the co-op could receive personalized, dynamic predictions of their own risk factors and current pregnancy status. Or customized advice on how to cope with morning sickness (a very misleading branding for all-day misery) or the constant fatigue.

By tapping into different data sources, the model could form a holistic impression of the mother's circumstances. Who is she (e.g., age, ethnicity, historical health records, levels of physical activity)? What's her social context like (e.g., Is she a single mom? Does she have a lot of support from other family members)? And what's the potential impact of her environment (e.g., Does she live in an urban area with high levels of air pollution)? Combining all these factors, is there anything our expectant mother should be worried about? And if so, what should she do? I would have signed up for this data co-op in a heartbeat.

You could think of many, many more examples. I've only listed a few here:

- Patients with rare diseases sharing their genetic information, medical history, and biometric data to improve our understanding of the disease and develop treatment options

- Professional or semiprofessional athletes trying to optimize their performance based on biometric feedback

- Women from underrepresented minorities pooling their genetic data to better understand the effectiveness of drugs that have been predominantly tested on white men

- Teachers pooling their classroom data and student performance to identify winning strategies for classroom engagement

What is common to all these examples is that the individuals involved voluntarily share a selection of their personal data with the co-op to help the entire co-op benefit from the group's insights. Having access to my own genetic data is useless if I am trying to figure out how to improve my pregnancy experience or the health of my future child. But it could be extremely valuable when pooled with the genetic data of other expectant mothers.

Data co-ops turn the existing data model upside down. Instead of a few companies controlling and profiting from your data, *you* decide who to share your data with and *you* benefit from doing so. This works because data co-ops (and data trusts) are owned by their members and bear fiduciary responsibilities. They are legally obligated to act in the best interests of their members. And because co-ops are effectively governed by their members, anyone who joins the crew gains partial control over how the co-op is run. The system runs on collective rights and accountability, as opposed to exploitation and obfuscation.

This shift in the ownership and incentive model makes co-ops ideal champions for the privacy-preserving technologies I introduced in the previous chapter. Federated learning wasn't developed specifically for data co-ops, but these organizations could be among its early adopters because they have a strong incentive to use such technology. This is unlike Facebook, which profits from accessing as much user data as possible. That's its business model. Data co-ops are the exact opposite. They act on behalf of their members and are measured by how successful they are in amplifying the benefits and mitigating the risks.

The specific goals of any given data co-op can vary. For example, some co-ops might focus on helping individuals monetize their data. Much like our wine co-op enhanced the returns on our grapes, data co-ops boost your bargaining power. With 20 million allies, the big players will suddenly have to take you seriously.

But monetizing data is just one of many potential goals of data co-ops and perhaps the least compelling. Data offers insights that can improve our lives and those of others. I would not sell my medical records for additional cash in my bank account (fully realizing that this is a privileged position to be in). But I would happily give it to a trustworthy organization focused on improving the health and well-being of expectant mothers and their babies. For free.

Let's look at some examples of what data co-ops might look like in practice. Although the concept is still relatively new, there are already several success stories.

There's the Driver's Seat Cooperative, a ride-hailing app that allows drivers to share their route data with one another and benefit from the collective insights this data can generate. What's the fastest route for this delivery? What's the best spot to pick up customers at 2 a.m.?

There's also the Swash co-op, which pays its members for browsing the internet by aggregating and selling web activities in a privacy-preserving way (with full control of each member over what data is collected).

And then there's my personal favorite: the Swiss data co-op MIDATA.

Changing the Swiss Health-Care Landscape

MIDATA was established as a nonprofit in 2015 by a group of scientists at ETH Zürich and the University of Applied Sciences in Bern (aka, my next-door village neighbors). The co-op acts as a trustee for its members, who can contribute to medical research and clinical studies by granting access to their personal health data on a case-by-case basis. Think of it like a bank account for health.

Anyone can open an account and deposit copies of their medical records or any type of health data that is valuable in this context (e.g., smartphone sensing data). MIDATA makes sure your data is securely stored in its collective vault and gives you full control over its use; you decide who to grant access, to which particular type of data, and for what purposes. And you can withdraw your personal data at any point in time.

But unlike your typical bank account, MIDATA isn't interested in generating profits (no ludicrous late fees). Its sole purpose is to maximize value for you and its other members. Any net profits that are generated from the use of your data get reinvested into making the services on the platform better (i.e., advances in data protection and technological developments). Similarly, as a member of MIDATA, you aren't just a bank customer. You own the bank. Literally. Control at MIDATA not only means control over your personal data. It also means having a direct say in the co-op's governance through a general assembly (so Swiss!).

The value MIDATA generates for its members takes different shapes. You can share access to your data with third parties to improve your own health. For example, there are personalized applications to help members overcome addiction or fight obesity. But you can also share your data to support scientific discovery, for example, to help researchers better understand allergies, food sensitivities, or rare disease. In many cases, the same application does both.

Take MiTrendS, an application that drives the scientific exploration and personalized treatment of multiple sclerosis (MS). MS is a chronic autoimmune disease that affects the central nervous system and cannot be cured (yet). By eating away the protective layer of nerve fiber in the brain, spinal cord, and optic nerves, MS significantly impacts patients' quality of life. They might have trouble seeing, experience fatigue, have a hard time concentrating and remembering things, and struggle with balance and tremor. A vicious combination of symptoms that often makes it difficult—if not impossible—for MS patients to thrive and fully engage in social life.

Although MS affects over 2.5 million people around the world, the disease remains hard to diagnose and even harder to treat. All we know is that MS is driven by a complex combination of infectious, genetic, and environmental factors. Because every patient has their

own unique set of symptoms and factors that contribute to the out-
break, understanding the disease and developing targeted treatments requires large amounts of data. Not just data from a lot of
patients, but also data from a lot of different sources: genetic data,
medical history, exposure to environmental risk factors, medication,
progression of symptoms over time, and more.

MiTrendS empowers patients and doctors to do just that. The app
allows users to track their symptoms over time from the comfort of
their home. For example, the app might ask you to follow a line on
your tablet with your finger as quickly and exactly as possible to
test your fine motor skills. Or match numbers to shapes to assess
your attention and concentration. By combining these symptom
assessments with existing patient records (i.e., medical records, medication information, brain scans, blood analyses, and more), MiTrendS
can develop personalized treatments and care plans for each patient,
a revolutionary approach that could change how MS is diagnosed and
treated.

Of course, the big pharma companies might occasionally invest in
large data collection efforts or buy patient data from hospitals to study
the disease. MS medication is expensive, and there's money to be
made. For the pharma companies, that is, of course. Not for the
patients whose data is used. In the best case, these patients will end
up paying for the medication. In the worst case, they will never get
to reap any benefits themselves.

The MiTrendS application turns this model upside down. By sharing their data, patients help develop better treatments for the future.
But they also directly benefit from more customized and targeted
treatment in the here and now.

Once a patient's data is securely stored and combined on the
MIDATA servers, a machine learning algorithm developed by researchers at ETH Zürich creates an optimal, personalized treatment plan
for them. The algorithm not only considers the patient's unique circumstances, but also leverages the insights obtained from all the
other MS patients on the platform (with their explicit consent).

After the algorithm spits out a recommendation, it is passed on to the MS specialists at the university hospitals that care for the patients. These specialists both implement the suggested treatment and provide feedback to the algorithm. Treatment X worked for patient A, but didn't work for patient B. It's the perfect feedback loop to continuously improve the algorithm's predictions and, with it, the care that can be offered to patients, a truly inspiring example of personalized medicine (which I touched on earlier, in chapter 6).

But there's more I love about MiTrendS. It involves the entire (local) community in its mission. That includes patients with MS, of course. But it also includes healthy individuals who can use the app to help researchers establish reliable data for comparison.

You can't understand a disease without tracking a patient's symptoms. How do their neurological impairments progress over time? Are they able to complete certain cognitive tasks, and how well? But you also can't understand a disease without having a clear sense of what to expect if those people weren't suffering from MS. How well would regular people do at the task? How quickly do they get tired?

That's what the MiTrendS citizen science part of the application does. It makes the village come together to support its most vulnerable members.

Making Data Co-ops a Viable Option

When I first heard of data co-ops a couple of years back, I immediately loved the concept. It sounded like a powerful approach to regaining all the fundamental rights we had lost in the transition to the digital economy. Privacy, transparency, self-determination. Data co-ops were designed to empower all of us; to not only take back control over our personal data and lives, but also benefit from the enormous value the digital economy had created (for a few big players rather than all of us).

As much as I love the concept of data co-ops, implementing them at scale is far from trivial. It requires us to fundamentally rethink the data ownership model and create an infrastructure that facilitates the collective management of personal data. But I am optimistic, mainly because we have pulled off similar stunts before.

When the Industrial Revolution concentrated power in the hands of a few major players, many citizens felt exploited and powerless. Over time, however, communities of individuals came together to form trade unions and citizen organizations that were guided by common interests and the desire to provide a counterweight to the big players.

Starting in the 1940s, for example, small member-owned electric cooperatives united under the umbrella of the National Rural Electric Cooperative Association to stand up against the energy giants of the time. Today, these cooperatives own over 40 percent of the electric infrastructure in the United States, covering more than 75 percent of the country. Not a bad outcome for people who started with no power at all.

Similarly, credit unions formed in response to the shift from traditional cash-based barter to digital consumer banking. When banks like J.P.Morgan threatened to dominate the market and exploit people for their own benefit, credit unions popped up all over the country. As nonprofit organizations with fiduciary responsibilities to their members, they started to offer many of the same financial services as traditional banks—minus the exploitation. Today, there are about 5,000 official credit unions in the United States servicing over 130 million individuals. That's more than one in every three Americans.

The two examples show that shifting power back to the people is possible in principle. However, what makes me so optimistic about them is that they could lay the foundations of data co-ops.

As two MIT professors, Alex (Sandy) Pentland and Thomas Hardjono, have convincingly argued, credit or trade unions could be among the first and largest data co-ops.[1] If you already entrust an entity to keep the lights on at home, negotiate your labor rights, or manage your investments and retirement fund, why not also entrust it with your personal data? It's the simplest way to give millions of people access to a trustworthy advocate for their personal data, practically overnight. Or as Pentland and Hardjono phrased it in a joint report with multiples such unions, leveraging existing trade unions could make the "widespread deployment of data cooperative capabilities . . . surprisingly quick and easy."

Regulatory environments—such as the European Union—which have already shifted data ownership to individuals by regulating data reuse and deletion, data interoperability, and portability, offer the ideal breeding ground for data co-ops. Your data is much more valuable when your data co-op is the only entity with access to it. As I mentioned in the previous chapter, bargaining becomes a lot harder if not only you have a copy of your data but everybody else does as well. It's the combination of a competent crew and a relatively tame sea that enables you to make the most of your personal data.

Most importantly, however, a competent crew is valuable even when the sea is still rough. In fact, that's perhaps when you need it the most—when sailing your boat alone is unlikely to end well.

Most US citizens don't currently own their data. If you have ever tried to get access to some of the digital traces you generate, you'll know how difficult (or even impossible) a task that is. In most parts of the United States, companies aren't legally required to share your own personal data with you. At the same time, companies have the right to use, share, and sell your data to any paying third-party entity without notifying you (and these third parties, in turn, are allowed to do the same).[2] Not a good spot to be in as a consumer. Left to your own devices, you have little to no power. Nobody is going to pick up your call and listen to your complaints and demands. But now imagine getting calls from millions of union members who are represented by expert lawyers. I bet someone is going to listen.

The Moral Imperative to Shape Our Future

F inding better ways of managing our personal data will be critical in the coming years and decades.

What I have described in *Mindmasters* is merely the tip of the iceberg. Technology is evolving at light speed. It's not just the growing amount of data we generate but also the increasingly sophisticated ways to analyze it that should give us pause and encourage us to rethink our current approach. Soon, we might have microbots in our blood that continuously scan our bodies for any sign of irregularity or disease, smart contact lenses that capture what we see and hyperpersonalize our views, and chips in our brain that not only read our thoughts but change them.

Sounds like science fiction? It isn't. Microbots and smart lenses are already a reality waiting to go mainstream. And the chips in our brain aren't so far off either. Neuroscientists are getting better and better at speaking the language of the brain. They have uncovered ways to project your thoughts on screens and explored different ways of altering your brain's wiring.[1]

Some of this research happens in academic institutions. But most of it is funded by powerful private entities that are just as interested in the commercialization of such technology as they are in scientific discovery. Leading the pack is Elon Musk, whose company Neuralink is tirelessly working toward this future.[2]

Everything I have discussed in *Mindmasters* pales in comparison to a world where third parties don't need to rely on psychological inferences from digital footprints anymore but directly access them at the source in our most secretive vault.

As we enter this world, we will learn more about the human psyche than ever before. We will create new opportunities to support the health and well-being of individuals and societies. Just imagine what preventive health care could look like if the microbots in our bloodstream detect the earliest signs of cancer long before any doctor could ever diagnose the disease. How we could augment our physical world with information projected directly onto our retinas to pique our curiosity and inspire awe. Or how we could not just step into the digital shoes of someone else but recreate their actual experience of the world in our own brains.

At the same time, we will face unprecedented challenges that threaten the very foundation of what makes us human. If we let third parties project their preferred version of our reality onto our retinas, how can we sustain a common foundation of what we collectively believe about the world around us? And if we allow others direct access to our brains, how will we know where a thought originated and whether it's truly ours? The last decade has seen growing concerns about digital ecosystems amplifying discrimination, polarization, echo chambers, and misinformation. If we continue our current trajectory, the next few decades could very well lead to the collapse of society as we know it.

Imagining the two sides of the same future creates a moral imperative to rethink the current data environment. We need a new social contract that defines what sharing our lives with others means in today's data-driven world. But rethinking the current data environment isn't enough. We need to recreate it. All of us. It doesn't matter whether you manage personal data for a living, or whether you are sick of the power imbalance the digital economy has created. We all have a role to play.

As I have suggested, returning to the village could be a solution. I'm not talking about physical villages or a model of the past we have moved beyond. I'm talking about a version of a village that is far superior to anything we have seen before. Growing up in Vögisheim, I had to live with both the advantages and disadvantages of letting other people into my life. I gradually got better at amplifying the good and downplaying the bad, but I had no hope of changing the system altogether. Living in today's digital village, we do. We have a unique opportunity to reclaim control over our lives and create a collective data infrastructure that benefits all of us.

Personality Test

Let's get started with figuring out your Big Five personality profile.[1]

First, you will need to answer a few questions about yourself. In the following table, I have noted several characteristics that may apply to you to various degrees. Some of them might be very close to how you see yourself, and others might be quite far. There are no right or wrong answers. The only purpose of this test is to help you understand your own personality profile.

There's no need to overthink your responses; the first one that comes to mind is usually the best. To mark your response, just put the number that best captures how you see yourself in the blank space next to each question.

Disagree strongly 1	Disagree moderately 2	Disagree a little 3	Neither agree nor disagree 4	Agree a little 5	Agree moderately 6	Agree strongly 7

I see myself as:

1. _____ Extroverted, enthusiastic

2. _____ Critical, quarrelsome

3. _____ Dependable, self-disciplined

4. _____ Anxious, easily upset

5. _____ Open to new experiences, complex

6. _____ Reserved, quiet

7. _____ Sympathetic, warm

8. _____ Disorganized, careless

9. _____ Calm, emotionally stable

10. _____ Conventional, uncreative

Source: Samuel D. Gosling, Peter J. Rentfrow, and William B. Swann Jr., "A Very Brief Measure of the Big Five Personality Domains," *Journal of Research in Personality* 37 (2003): 504–528.

Done? Here's how to score the test. There are two questions for each of the five personality traits. Say you score yourself a 5 on question 1 and a 2 on question 6, your extroversion score would be $5 + (8 - 2) = 11$. The next table shows you which questions belong to which trait.

Openness	=	Score on question 5 + (8 – score on question 10)
Conscientiousness	=	Score on question 3 + (8 – score on question 8)
Extroversion	=	Score on question 1 + (8 – score on question 6)
Agreeableness	=	Score on question 7 + (8 – score on question 2)
Neuroticism	=	Score on question 4 + (8 – score on question 9)

Got your scores? Great! But wait a second, what does it mean to have a score of 5.5 on extroversion? Is that high or low? You will notice

FIGURE A-1

Average scores for Big Five personality traits

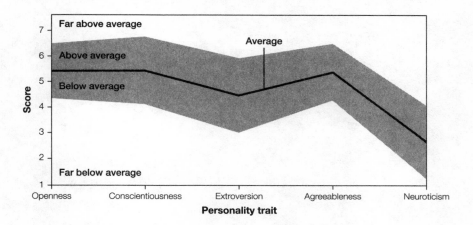

Source: Samuel D. Gosling, Peter J. Rentfrow, and William B. Swann Jr., "A Very Brief Measure of the Big Five Personality Domains," *Journal of Research in Personality* 37, no. 6 (2003): 504–528.

that the scores you just calculated don't mean much without any context. To make sense of them, we need to compare your scores to those of other people (in this case, thousands of people who have taken the same test before).

I have plotted the average for each trait in figure A-1, along with bands that indicate how extreme your score might be. You can take the scores you calculated and transfer them as crosses into the graph (if you want a more detailed profile, I recommend taking the test on our dedicated website www.mindmasters.ai/mypersonality).

APPENDIX B

We didn't get to explore the relationships of Facebook likes and status updates for all the five personality traits in the main book. But here they are. Table B-1 lists Facebook likes related to these traits, while figure B-1 depicts words in people's Facebook status updates indicative of these same traits. Just like the lists of likes and word clouds for extroversion and agreeableness in chapter 2, the ones for openness, conscientiousness, and neuroticism showcase how intuitive many of the links between our online behaviors and psychological characteristics are.

Facebook likes related to openness, conscientiousness, and neuroticism

Personality trait	Low	High
Openness	NASCAR	Oscar Wilde
	Austin Collie	Charles Bukowski
	Monster-in-Law	Leonardo da Vinci
	I don't read	Bauhaus
	Justin Moore	*Dmt: The Spirit Molecule*
	ESPN2	*American Gods*
	Farmlandia	John Waters
	The Bachelor	Plato
	Teen Mom 2	Leonard Cohen
Conscientiousness	Wes Anderson	Law officer
	Bandit Nation	National law enforcement
	Omegle	Lowfares.com
	Vocaloid	Accounting
	Serial Killer	Foursquare
	Screamo	Emergency medical services
	Anime	Sunday Best
	Vamplets	Kaplan University
	Join If Ur Fat	Glock Inc
	Not Dying	MyCalendar 2010
Neuroticism	Business administration	Sometimes I hate myself
	Getting money	Emo
	Parkour	*Girl Interrupted*
	Track and field	SO SO Happy
	Skydiving	*The Addams Family*
	Mountain biking	Vocaloid
	Soccer	Sixbillionsecrets.com
	Climbing	*Vampires Everywhere*
	Physics/engineering	Kurt Donald Cobain
	48 Laws of Power	Dot Dot Curve

Facebook status updates related to openness, conscientiousness, and neuroticism

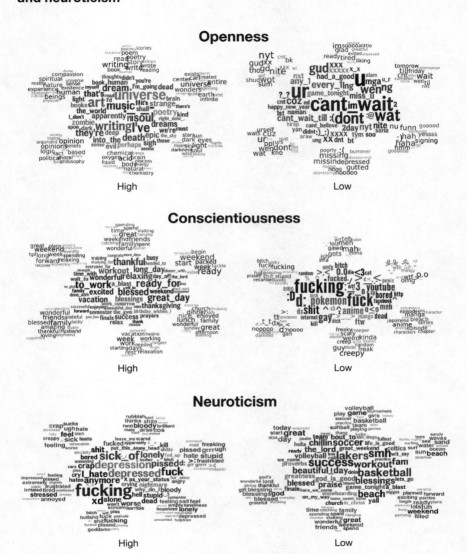

Openness

High

Low

Conscientiousness

High

Low

Neuroticism

High

Low

Scan the QR code for a color version of the word clouds.

Source: H. Andrew Schwartz et al., "Personality, Gender, and Age in the Language of Social Media: The Open-Vocabulary Approach," *PLoS One* 8, no. 9 (2013): e73791, https://doi.org/10.1371/journal.pone.0073791. Permission via https://creativecommons.org/licenses/by/4.0/.

NOTES

Introduction

1. Michael Reilly, "Is Facebook Targeting Ads at Sad Teens?," *MIT Technology Review*, May 1, 2017, https://www.technologyreview.com/2017/05/01/105987/is-facebook-targeting-ads-at-sad-teens.

2. Melvin Kranzberg, "Technology and History: 'Kranzberg's Laws,'" *Technology and Culture* 27, no. 3 (July 1986): 544–560.

Chapter 1

1. "Data Never Sleeps," DOMO, 2018, https://www.domo.com/solution/data-never-sleeps-6.

2. Youyou Wu, Michal Kosinski, and David Stillwell, "Computer-based Personality Judgments Are More Accurate Than Those Made by Humans," *Proceedings of the National Academy of Sciences* 112, no. 4 (2015): 1036–1040.

3. Gerald Matthews, Ian J. Deary, and Martha C. Whiteman, *Personality Traits* (Cambridge, UK: Cambridge University Press, 2003).

Chapter 2

1. Diana I. Tamir and Jason P. Mitchell, "Disclosing Information about the Self Is Intrinsically Rewarding," *Proceedings of the National Academy of Sciences* 109, no. 21 (2012): 8038–8043.

2. Mor Naaman, Jeffrey Boase, and Chih-Hui Lai, "Is It Really about Me? Message Content in Social Awareness Streams," *Proceedings of the 2010 ACM Conference on Computer Supported Cooperative Work*, February 2010, 189–192.

3. Mitja D. Back et al., "Facebook Profiles Reflect Actual Personality, not Self-Idealization," *Psychological Science* 21, no. 3 (2010): 372–374.

4. Yoko Akiyoshi, "Retired Japanese Police Officer Sets New Hello Kitty Record," NBC News, July 4, 2017, https://www.nbcnews.com/news/world/retired-japanese-police-officer-sets-new-hello-kitty-record-n779476.

5. Michal Kosinski, David Stillwell, and Thore Graepel, "Private Traits and Attributes Are Predictable from Digital records of Human Behavior," *Proceedings of the National Academy of Sciences* 110, no. 15 (2013): 5802–5805.

6. James W. Pennebaker, *The Secret Life of Pronouns* (New York: Bloomsbury Publishing USA, 2013).

7. Allison M. Tackman et al., "Depression, Negative Emotionality, and Self-referential Language: A Multi-lab, Multi-measure, and Multi-language-task Research Synthesis," *Journal of Personality and Social Psychology* 116, no. 5 (2019): 817.

8. Johannes C. Eichstaedt et al., "Facebook Language Predicts Depression in Medical Records," *Proceedings of the National Academy of Sciences* 115, no. 44 (2018): 11203–11208.

9. Jonathan Timm, "When the Boss Says 'Don't Tell Your Coworkers How Much You Get Paid," *Atlantic*, July 15, 2014, https://www.theatlantic.com/business/archive/2014/07/when-the-boss-says-dont-tell-your-coworkers-how-much-you-get-paid/374467/.

10. Sandra C. Matz et al., "Predicting Individual-level Income from Facebook Profiles," *PloS One* 14, no. 3 (2019): e0214369.

11. Cristina Segalin et al., "The Pictures We Like Are Our Image: Continuous Mapping of Favorite Pictures into Self-assessed and Attributed Personality Traits," *IEEE Transactions on Affective Computing* 8, no. 2 (2016): 268–285.

12. Yilun Wang and Michal Kosinski, "Deep Neural Networks Are More Accurate Than Humans at Detecting Sexual Orientation from Facial Images," *Journal of Personality and Social Psychology* 114, no. 2 (2018): 246.

13. Aaron W. Lukaszewski and James R. Roney, "The Origins of Extraversion: Joint Effects of Facultative Calibration and Genetic Polymorphism," *Personality and Social Psychology Bulletin* 37 (2011): 409–421.

Chapter 3

1. Sam Gosling, *Snoop: What Your Stuff Says about You* (New York: Basic Books, 2008).

2. Seth Stephens-Davidowitz, *Everybody Lies: Big Data, New Data, and What the Internet Can Tell Us About Who We Really Are* (New York: Dey Street Books, 2017).

3. Laokoon, *Made to Measure: A Digital Search for Traces*, 2020, https://www.madetomeasure.online/en/.

4. Yves-Alexandre de Montjoye et al., "Unique in the Shopping Mall: On the Reidentifiability of Credit Card Metadata," *Science* 347, no. 6221 (2015): 536–539.

5. Joe J. Gladstone, Sandra C. Matz, and Alain Lemaire, "Can Psychological Traits Be Inferred from Spending? Evidence from Transaction Data," *Psychological Science* 30, no. 7 (2019): 1087–1096.

6. Jessie London, "How Jaila Gladden's iPhone Saved Her Life," Medium, January 21, 2021, https://jessielondon.medium.com/how-jaila-gladdens-iphone-saved-her-life-48d0c285d147.

7. Shiri Melumad and Michel Tuan Pham, "The Smartphone as a Pacifying Technology," *Journal of Consumer Research* 47, no. 2 (2020): 237–255.

8. Clemens Stachl et al., "Predicting Personality from Patterns of Behavior Collected with Smartphones," *Proceedings of the National Academy of Sciences* 117, no. 30 (2020): 17680–17687.

9. Sandrine R. Müller et al., "Depression Predictions from GPS-based Mobility Do Not Generalize Well to Large Demographically Heterogeneous Samples," *Scientific Reports* 11, no. 1 (2021): 14007.

Chapter 4

1. William Fleeson, "Toward a Structure- and Process-Integrated View of Personality: Traits as Density Distributions of States," *Journal of Personality and Social Psychology* 80, no. 6 (2001): 1011.

2. Robert E. Wilson, Renee J. Thompson, and Simine Vazire, "Are Fluctuations in Personality States More Than Fluctuations in Affect?," *Journal of Research in Personality* 69 (2017): 110–123.

3. Sandra C. Matz and Gabriella M. Harari, "Personality–Place Transactions: Mapping the Relationships between Big Five Personality Traits, States, and Daily Places," *Journal of Personality and Social Psychology* 120, no. 5 (2021): 1367.

4. Andrew B. Blake et al., "Wearable Cameras, Machine Vision, and Big Data Analytics: Insights into People and the Places They Go," In *Big Data in Psychological Research*, S. E. Woo, L. Tay, and R. W. Proctor, eds., (Washington, DC: American Psychological Association, 2020), 125–143.

5. John F. Rauthmann et al., "The Situational Eight DIAMONDS: A Taxonomy of Major Dimensions of Situation Characteristics," *Journal of Personality and Social Psychology* 107, no. 4 (2014): 677.

6. Ramona Schoedel et al., "Snapshots of Daily Life: Situations Investigated through the Lens of Smartphone Sensing," *Journal of Personality and Social Psychology* 125, no. 6 (2023): 1442–1471.

7. Heinrich Peters and Sandra Matz, "Large Language Models Can Infer Psychological Dispositions of Social Media Users," *PNAS Nexus* 3, no. 6 (2024), https://academic.oup.com/pnasnexus/article/3/6/pgae231/7692212.

Chapter 5

1. Hannes Grassegger and Mikael Krogerus, "Ich habe nur gezeigt, dass es die Bombe gibt (I Just Showed That the Bomb Exists)," *TA International*, March 20, 2018, https://www.tagesanzeiger.ch/ich-habe-nur-gezeigt-dass-es-die-bombe-gibt-652492646668.

2. Hannes Grassegger and Mikael Krogerus, "The Data That Turned the World Upside Down," Motherboard, January 28, 2017, https://www.vice.com/en/article/mg9vvn/how-our-likes-helped-trump-win.

3. Harry Davies, "Ted Cruz Using Firm That Harvested Data on Millions of Unwitting Facebook Users," *Guardian*, December 11, 2015, https://www.theguardian.com/us-news/2015/dec/11/senator-ted-cruz-president-campaign-facebook-user-data.

4. Michal Kosinski, David Stillwell, and Thore Graepel, "Private Traits and Attributes Are Predictable from Digital Records of Human Behavior," *Proceedings of the National Academy of Sciences* 110, no. 15 (2013): 5802–5805.

5. "Hilton Launches Holiday Matchmaking App," Breaking Travel News, July 14, 2015, https://www.breakingtravelnews.com/news/article/hilton-launches-holiday-matchmaking-app/.

6. Sidney J. Levy, "Symbols for Sale," *Harvard Business Review*, July–August 1959, 117–124.

7. Sandra C. Matz et al., "Psychological Targeting as an Effective Approach to Digital Mass Persuasion," *Proceedings of the National Academy of Sciences* 114, no. 48 (2017): 12714–12719.

8. Sandra C. Matz et al., "Predicting the Personal Appeal of Marketing Images Using Computational Methods," *Journal of Consumer Psychology* 29, no. 3 (2019): 370–390.

9. The quote is ChatGPT's response to author's question "Write an iPhone ad for someone who is extroverted and enthusiastic," obtained March 25, 2023, using OpenAI's GPT-3 playground.

10. Sandra Matz et al., "The Potential of Generative AI for Personalized Persuasion at Scale," *Scientific Reports* 14, no. 1 (2023): 4692.

11. Jonathan Haidt and Craig Joseph, "The Moral Mind: How Five Sets of Innate Intuitions Guide the Development of Many Culture-specific Virtues, and Perhaps Even Modules," *The Innate Mind* 3 (2007): 367–391.

12. Jesse Graham, Jonathan Haidt, and Brian A. Nosek, "Liberals and Conservatives Rely on Different Sets of Moral Foundations," *Journal of Personality and Social Psychology* 96, no. 5 (2009): 1029.

13. Matthew Feinberg and Robb Willer, "Moral Reframing: A Technique for Effective and Persuasive Communication across Political Divides," *Social and Personality Psychology Compass* 13, no. 12 (2019): e12501.

14. Feinberg and Willer, "Moral Reframing"; Matz, et al., "Predicting the Personal Appeal of Marketing Images."

15. Jennifer Nancy Lee Allen, Duncan J. Watts, and David Rand, "Quantifying the Impact of Misinformation and Vaccine-Skeptical Content on Facebook," PsyArXiv, September 9, 2023, doi:10.31234/osf.io/nwsqa.

Chapter 6

1. Sandra C. Matz, Joe J. Gladstone, and David Stillwell, "Money Buys Happiness When Spending Fits Our Personality," *Psychological Science* 27, no. 5 (2016): 715–725.

2. Ann Carrns, "Even in Strong Economy, Most Families Don't Have Enough Emergency Savings," *New York Times*, October 25, 2019, https://www.nytimes.com/2019/10/25/your-money/emergency-savings.html.

3. Sendhil Mullainathan and Eldar Shafir, *Scarcity: Why Having Too Little Means So Much* (New York: Macmillan, 2013).

4. Carrns, "Even in Strong Economy, Most Families Don't Have Enough Emergency Savings."

5. Sandra C. Matz, and Joe J. Gladstone, "Nice Guys Finish Last: When and Why Agreeableness Is Associated with Economic Hardship," *Journal of Personality and Social Psychology* 118, no. 3 (2020): 545.

6. Sandra C. Matz, Joe J. Gladstone, and Robert A. Farrokhnia, "Leveraging Psychological Fit to Encourage Saving Behavior," *American Psychologist* 78, no. 7 (2023): 901–917.

7. Copyright © 2023 by the American Psychological Association. Reproduced by permission. Sandra C. Matz, Joe J. Gladstone, and Robert A. Farrokhnia, "Leveraging Psychological Fit to Encourage Saving Behavior," *American Psychologist* 78, no. 7 (2023): 901–917.

8. My eternal gratitude and admiration go to the SaverLife creative team that pulled off this stunt before ChatGPT was a thing!

9. Sam Levin, "Facebook Told Advertisers It Can Identify Teens Feeling 'Insecure' and 'Worthless,'" *Guardian*, May 1, 2017, https://www.theguardian.com/technology/2017/may/01/facebook-advertising-data-insecure-teens.

10. Sung Jun Park et al., "New Paradigm for Tumor Theranostic Methodology Using Bacteria-based Microrobot," *Scientific Reports* 3, no. 1 (2013): 3394.

11. Robert Lewis et al., "Can a Recommender System Support Treatment Personalisation in Digital Mental Health Therapy? A Quantitative Feasibility Assessment Using Data from a Behavioural Activation Therapy App," in *CHI Conference on Human Factors in Computing Systems Extended Abstracts* (2022), 1–8.

12. Yuki Nogucki, "Therapy by Chatbot? The Promise and Challenges in Using AI for Mental Health," *Shots*, NPR, January 19, 2023, https://www.npr.org/sections

/health-shots/2023/01/19/1147081115/therapy-by-chatbot-the-promise-and
-challenges-in-using-ai-for-mental-health.

13. Nick Zagorski, "Popularity of Mental Health Chatbots Grows," *Psychiatric News* 57, no. 5 (2022), https://psychnews.psychiatryonline.org/doi/10.1176/appi.pn .2022.05.4.50.

14. Eli J. Finkel et al., "Political Sectarianism in America," *Science* 370, no. 6516 (2020): 533–536.

15. Thomas H. Costello, Gordon Pennycook, and David Rand, "Durably Reducing Conspiracy Beliefs through Dialogues with AI," PsyArXiv, April 3, 2024, doi:10.31234 /osf.io/xcwdn.

Chapter 7

1. Paul Mozur, Muyi Xiao, and John Liu, "'An Invisible Cage': How China Is Policing the Future," *New York Times*, June 25, 2022, https://www.nytimes.com/2022 /06/25/technology/china-surveillance-police.html.

2. Paul Mozur, Muyi Xiao, and John Liu, "'An Invisible Cage.'"

3. "Sun on Privacy: 'Get Over It,'" *Wired*, January 26, 1999, https://www.wired .com/1999/01/sun-on-privacy-get-over-it/.

4. Eileen Guo, "A Roomba Recorded a Woman on the Toilet. How Did Screen-shots End Up on Facebook?," *MIT Technology Review*, December 19, 2022, https:// www.technologyreview.com/2022/12/19/1065306/roomba-irobot-robot-vacuums -artificial-intelligence-training-data-privacy/.

5. Amanda Reill, "A Simple Way to Make Better Decisions," hbr.org, December 6, 2023, https://hbr.org/2023/12/a-simple-way-to-make-better-decisions.

Chapter 8

1. Chris Jay Hoofnagle and Jennifer M. Urban, "Alan Westin's Privacy Homo Economicus," *Wake Forest Law Review* 49 (2014): 261.

2. Azim Shariff, Joe Green, and William Jettinghoff, "The Privacy Mismatch: Evolved Intuitions in a Digital World," *Current Directions in Psychological Science* 30, no. 2 (2021): 159–166.

3. Alessandro Acquisti, Laura Brandimarte, and George Loewenstein, "Privacy and Human Behavior in the Age of Information," *Science* 347, no. 6221 (2015): 509–514.

Chapter 9

1. Eric J. Johnson and Daniel G. Goldstein, "Do Defaults Save Lives?," *Science* 302, no. 5649 (2003): 1338–1339.

2. Aristotle, *The Nicomachian Ethics of Aristotle*, tenth edition, trans. F. H. Peters (London: Kegan Paul, Trench, Trübner and Co., 1906), 289.

3. Alessandro Acquisti, Leslie K. John, and George Loewenstein, "What Is Privacy Worth?," *Journal of Legal Studies* 42, no. 2 (2013): 249–274.

4. Peter Kairouz et al., "Advances and Open Problems in Federated Learning," *Foundations and Trends in Machine Learning* 14, no. 1–2 (2021): 1–210.

5. Cory Doctorow, "Personal Data Is as Hot as Nuclear Waste," *Guardian*, January 15, 2008, https://www.theguardian.com/technology/2008/jan/15/data .security.

6. Nina Totenberg, "An Attacker Killed a Judge's Son. Now She Want to Protect Other Families," NPR, November 20, 2020, https://www.npr.org/2020/11/20 /936717194/a-judge-watched-her-son-die-now-she-wants-to-protect-other-judicial -families.

7. The Daniel Anderl Judicial Security and Privacy Act, The Courts and Congress Annual Report 2022, https://www.uscourts.gov/statistics-reports/courts-and -congress-annual-report-2022.

8. Roger McNamee, *Zucked: Waking Up to the Facebook Catastrophe* (New York: Penguin, 2020).

Chapter 10

1. Alex Pentland and Thomas Hardjono, "Data Cooperatives," in *Building the New Economy* (Cambridge, MA: MIT Press, 2020), https://wip.mitpress.mit.edu/pub /pnxgvubq/release/2.

2. Thorin Klosowski, "The State of Consumer Data Privacy Laws in the US (And Why It Matters)," Wirecutter, *New York Times*, September 6, 2021, https://www .nytimes.com/wirecutter/blog/state-of-privacy-laws-in-us/.

Epilogue

1. Moran Cerf et al., "On-line, Voluntary Control of Human Temporal Lobe Neurons," *Nature* 467, no. 7319 (2010): 1104–1108.

2. Daniel Gilbert, "The Race to Beat Elon Musk to Put Chips in People's Brains," *Washington Post*, March 3, 2023, https://www.washingtonpost.com/business/2023 /03/03/brain-chips-paradromics-synchron/.

Appendix A

1. Samuel D. Gosling, Peter J. Rentfrow, and William B. Swann Jr., "A Very Brief Measure of the Big Five Personality Domains," *Journal of Research in Personality* 37 (2003): 504–528.

INDEX

ACKNOWLEDGMENTS

When I first started writing about my work in less academic terms, it wasn't with the intent of publishing a book. I simply wanted to help my friends and family understand what I was doing thousands of miles away from home, across the Atlantic. However, I soon fell in love with the conversational style of communicating my ideas and scientific findings. And I was fortunate to have an entire community supporting me in bringing this effort to fruition.

It's not just the people named here but also my wonderful collaborators and the remarkable researchers whose work has shaped my thinking and enriched so many passages throughout the book. Academic life can be lonely at times, but writing *Mindmasters* repeatedly reminded me of how lucky I am to be part of a community dedicated to pushing the envelope of knowledge and making a meaningful contribution to our collective wisdom.

Among just a few of those whose support carried me through this journey and whose brilliance is enshrined in the pages of this book, I want to first and foremost thank my agent, Leila Campoli. Without you, there would be no *Mindmasters*. You believed in me and my ideas from the beginning and gave me the confidence to move from writing stories for my parents to reaching (I hope) a much larger audience. I couldn't have asked for a more talented, kind, and supportive agent, and I am eternally grateful for your continued guidance and encouragement.

I also want to thank my editor, Kevin Evers, and the entire team at Harvard Business Review Press for helping me make this book a reality. Kevin, your enthusiasm for the book was contagious, and your keen eye for compelling stories has made *Mindmasters* far more entertaining than it otherwise would have been.

None of the work described in *Mindmasters* would have been possible without my wonderful students, colleagues, and mentors, who coauthored many of the papers referenced in the book. You are extraordinary scholars and true friends. The countless hours we spent working together in kitchens, libraries, coffee shops, parks, and offices (some nicer than others) encompass many of the most inspiring and happiest moments of my life. A special thanks to my coauthors (in alphabetical order): Ruth Appel, Erica Bailey, Maarten Bos, Moran Cerf, Brian Croll, Tobias Ebert, Robert Farrokhnia, Brandon Freiberg, Joe Gladstone, Friedrich Goetz, Sam Gosling, Gabriella Harari, Michal Kosinski, Asher Lawson, Ashley Martin, Sandrine Mueller, Gideon Nave, Heinrich Peters, Vess Popov, Jason Rentfrow, Andy Schwartz, Clemens Stachl, David Stillwell, Jake Teeny, Sumer Vaid, and Youyou Wu. You rock!

I am also incredibly grateful to my colleagues and students at Columbia Business School. For the last seven years, you have become family to me. I feel like the luckiest person in the world to have found work I love in a place that feels like home. A special shout-out to all the current and former members of the Computational Behavioral Science Lab, particularly Minhee Kim, whose support as a lab manager has been invaluable. I'm so honored to be part of your journey to becoming the next generation of academic thought leaders and educators. Thank you all!

Most importantly, I want to thank my family—my son, Ben, my mom and dad, my sister and her family, and my in-laws—for their unconditional love and support. You have always encouraged me to reach for the stars, no matter how far away they seemed. I wouldn't be where I am today without you. I took leaps of faith because I knew you had my back no matter what. I started writing this book for you, and I hope seeing it in print will make you proud and remind you of how much I love you.

Finally, I want to thank my partner in life and crime, Moran Cerf. You are my biggest inspiration, closest confidant, and favorite comedian. Your presence turns even the most mundane experience into an unforgettable adventure. It has not escaped my notice that you make me a better person every day.

ABOUT THE AUTHOR

SANDRA MATZ was born and raised in a small village in the southwest corner of Germany. After receiving her Bachelor of Science in psychology at the University of Freiburg and her PhD from the University of Cambridge, Matz joined Columbia Business School as a professor of business at the age of twenty-seven. She currently serves as the codirector of both the Leadership Lab and the Center for Advanced Technology and Human Performance.

As a computational social scientist with a background in psychology and computer science, Matz studies human behavior by uncovering the hidden relationships between our digital footprints and our inner mental lives. Her goal is to make data relatable and help individuals, businesses, and policymakers use data in more-effective and ethical ways.

Over the last ten years she has published more than fifty academic papers in the world's leading peer-reviewed journals, and her work has frequently been covered by many major news outlets, including the *Economist*, the *New York Times*, the *Wall Street Journal*, *Forbes*, and *Business Insider*. In addition, Matz has shared her findings with business leaders, policymakers, and the broader public through op-eds, keynote speeches, podcasts, TV appearances, and consulting work.

Matz has won numerous awards for her research and teaching, including the SAGE Early Career Trajectory Award for social and personality psychologists; Poets and Quants' Best 40-Under-40 MBA professors; *Capital* magazine's Young Elite Top 40 Under 40; World

Frontiers Forum Young Pioneers; *Pacific Standard* magazine's Top 30 Thinkers Under 30; and DataIQ's 100 Most Influential People in Data.

She lives in New York City with her husband, Moran Cerf, and her son, Ben Cerf.